# The Storyteller
# Tales from Tiger Mountain

## by Janie P. Taylor

To: Janie

Best wishes to a
lovely lady!

Blessings!

Janie P. Taylor

2009

ISBN 978-0-9799834-2-9
Library of Congress cataloging in progress.

The photographs of Tiger Mountain depicting
the four seasons: Winter, Spring, Summer, Fall,
were taken by Harry M. (Skip) Bartlett.
After a career as an educator and commercial
photographer, he and his wife, the former Lucy Ezzard,
retired to their home at the base of Tiger Mountain.
Skip now enjoys freelance photography and
recording the flora and fauna around his home
and throughout North Georgia.

Cover design by Tracy McCoy
Layout by Dianne VanderHorst
Illustrations by Dawne W. Bryan & Becky W. Ray
Reviewer - Peggy P. Thrasher

Published by

LAUREL
Mountain
PRESS
www.laurelmountainpress.com

P.O. Box 1973, Clayton, Georgia
Printed in the United States of America

*Dedicated to my loving family*
*and supportive friends.*

# Contents

# Chapter 1
## Treasures in the Trunk

# Treasures in the Trunk

Recently, the time had arrived that it became necessary to check the contents of a very old family trunk. After dusting and cleaning the trunk, we three siblings (Jim, Peggy, and I) slowly lifted the lid with the rusty hinges creaking and looked inside.

There were collections of photographs of every size and description of generations past; a hand-woven wool coverlet made by an Arrendale second cousin; a folded but faded wedding dress and veil; and tiny baby garments including a sacque, cap, and booties.

Then we spotted a long cardboard roll and an aged yellow folder. Closer inspection revealed a diploma belonging to our mother, Clyde Ellen Arrendale, from Young Harris College, dated May 24, 1926. She was only 18 years of age. Nearby was a copy of the college newspaper, "Enotah Echoes", which revealed that Mother was a commencement speaker.

Next, we opened the folder to discover, in her hand-writing, a manuscript entitled "The Mountaineer", which she had written, memorized, and delivered at the Young Harris College graduation exercise. This speech was so descriptive and so historically correct as to the background of us mountain people that Peggy, Jim, and I decided to share this speech with you, the reader.

# SENIOR EDITION

# The ENOTAH ECHOES

VOL. I. No. 10.                    YOUNG HARRIS, GA., MAY 20, 1926                    50c Per Term—$1.50 Per Year

## Dr. J. A. Sharp

President Young Harris College

### Dr. Sharp To Deliver Baccalaureate Address

On Monday evening, May 24, Dr. J. A. Sharp will deliver the Baccalaureate address. Most of the Seniors have been here for more than two years and they wished that the speaker of their program be their own President. And this is the greatest

## COMMENCEMENT PROGRAM

The Commencement Exercises will begin May 20th and extend through the 24th. The first of the series will be the presentation of Moliere's "Country Gentleman" Thursday evening, May 20th, Prof. Worth Sharp, head of the French department is directing the play.

Friday evening, May 21, Academy Graduating Exercises. Prof. W. O Payne will deliver the Baccalaurate address.

Saturday evening, May 22nd, the Young Harris and Phi Chi Literary and Debating societies will hold their annual champion Debate.

Sunday Morning, May 23rd, Dr. Plato Durham, of Emory University, will preach the Commencement sermon.

Sunday Evening, May 23nd, Rev. Clay Emory, of Milledgeville, Ga., will preach a special sermon to young people.

Monday a. m., May 24th, the Junior class will render its program. Dr. W. D. Hooper, of the University of Georgia, will deliver the literary address.

Monday evening, May 24th, the Senior class will close the series with

## Dr. W. D. Hooper To Deliver The Literary Address

Dr. W. D. Hooper, head of the Latin Department of the University of Georgia will deliver the Literary address of the commencement exercises, on Monday morning, May 24.

Dr. Hooper is one of the best known teachers in the state and is one of the best grammarians in the South. He is President of the Southern Association of Accredited High Schools and Colleges. Dr. Hooper's address will be one of the main features of the exercises and is looked forward to by the school. This is his first visit to Young Harris and we hope that he will consent to come to visit us again.

### Dr. Plato Durham Will Preach Sermon At Commencement

Dr. Plato Durham, of the faculty of Emory University, on Sunday May 23, will preach the Commencement Sermon. Dr. Durham is known throughout the South as one of the South's greatest preachers. His sermon will be an inspiration to the

## William Lawson Peel

Chairman Board of Trustees

Col. W. L. Peel, of Atlanta, is one of the greatest friends of our school. He gave to us a beautiful dormitory that is named in honor of him. He has helped many deserving young men and women to get an education.

4

"The Mountaineers"

by Clyde Arrendale, 1926, Young Harris College

In the southern part of the United States there is a chain of mighty mountains, the Appalachians, which, though much older and not so rugged as the corresponding Rockies of the west, presented a formidable barrier to the American pioneer. Lacking in rivers as pathways and with few passes, these southern ranges could not be crossed as the northern mountains could.

The only ones who dared to lose themselves in these 101,880 square miles of unexplored streams and ranges were the true pioneers, who cared not for loneliness or danger, who fared forth with a small pack of food, a musket rifle and an undaunted courage.

But the spirit of the pioneer is to ever move forward and search for the new, so families moved into the coves and valleys and began a life of struggle and hardship, while the tide of emigration swept on into the west.

These mountain settlers were mainly Scotch-Irish who fled from the oppressive James II and landed at Boston, Philadelphia, and

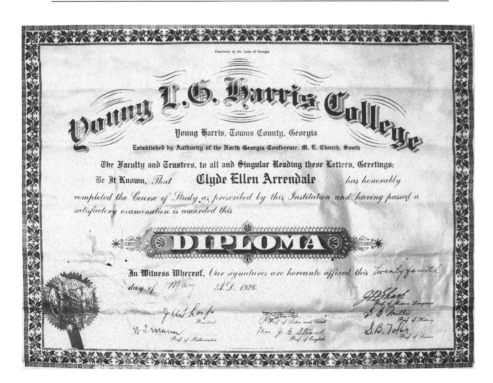

Charleston and drifted inland until they merged together in the mountains of North Georgia, Eastern Tennessee, Western Carolina, and Kentucky. They were mainly the same stock they were when they landed, but they had been joined by the French, German, and English Protestants who had fled from persecutions in Europe.

The late Theodore Roosevelt, in his "Winning of the West", pays the following tribute to these pioneers: "The backwoods men were Americans by birth and parentage, and of mixed race, but the dominant strain in their blood was that of Presbyterian Irish -- or the Scotch-Irish as they were often called. Full credit has been awarded the Roundhead and the Cavalier for their leadership in our history, nor have we altogether been blind to the deeds of the Hollander and Hugenots, but it is doubtful if we have wholly realized the importance of the part played by that stern and virile people, the Irish, whose preachers taught the creed of Knox and Calvin. These Irish representatives of the Covenauters were in the west almost what the Puritans were in the northeast and the Cavaliers were in the south. Mingled with the descendants of many other races, they formed the kernel of the distinctively and intensely American stock who were the pioneers of our people in their march westward."

While the rest of the nation was in a whirlpool of events, discoveries, inventions and new learning, these people in the backwater stood still, living their lives contented to let the protecting mountains be their stronghold against all outside affairs, for though he is friendly when you show yourself a friend, the mountaineer grows in soul, body and mind in the solitude of his beloved home.

The families were dependent on no one. They produced their own food, with the exception of a bit of salt, sugar, and coffee, which the head of the home swapped for his truck (surplus crops) on his yearly visit to the nearest town or city. The sheep were raised on the verdant pastures and the women carried the wool through each step of manufacture till the family wardrobe was complete.

The community life centered around the log church or meeting house and on preaching Sundays, the congregation would gather from miles around, coming by ox cart, mule back, or walking. But they came! For the mountaineer is conscientious in every respect. He is deeply religious, for each day he "lifts his eyes up unto the hills from which comes his strength".

The spirit of fellowship and goodwill was manifested in the log-rollings, where the men gathered to clear a plot of land and vied with each other in physical strength and endurance; in the house raisings, where each tried to build his corner of the house straighter than the others; in the reapings, where the man who could harvest the wheat the fastest led the group across the field; and in the corn-shuckings, where the champion was determined by the one who found the most colored ears of corn. While the men were working, the women would be cooking the bountiful dinner, quilting, sewing or knitting, while the older children cared for the younger ones. After the day's work was over, the young people would gather and have a singing, candy pulling, or where it was not banned, an old fashioned dance. For the mountain lads and lassies are as other lads and lassies the world over and the gayness, fun and companionship of youth was not neglected.

The education of the mountaineer has been woefully neglected, the families were scattered, the winters so rough and the money so scarce that it was impossible to have much more than a three month, one teacher school where only the blue-black speller was taught. But there were some who pressed forward and went out into the world and have made successes. For instance, Dr. George W. Truett, Judge Logan E Bleckley, our own Dr. Sharp, and many others. Still, many go out and receive an education and come back to help their own kindred out of the stagnant pool of ignorance and superstition.

And the mountaineers are awakening to the greatness of the future that is before them. Better systems of schools are being worked out so that more and more are receiving an education and the old community spirit is being revived again in cooperative projects and work which brings the people together with a common interest and an outstanding purpose. He is beginning to realize the wealth stored in these hills and he is by various means forcing the world to realize that the mountaineer is not a "mountain white" to be pitied, scorned, and feared but that he is of equal with any in intellect, initiative, leadership and business ability, yet with a noble trust in God and faith in his fellowman.

It has been said that for generations these mountains have been used as a storehouse for a nation in which God has kept untainted a race of strong-willed, strong-minded and strong bodied men, so that when the need comes, the mountaineer can answer the call of country, creed, or truth and fare forth as did the pioneer of old with his purpose to forge ahead and his undaunted courage, and surely the mountaineer is coming into his own and truly:

"Dear is that shed to which his soul conforms,
And dear that hill which lifts him to the storms,
So the loud torrent and the whirlwind's roar,
But bind him to his native mountains more".

As I read over and over, this speech which Mother had written, I realized that from her I had inherited my love for these mountains (and Tiger Mountain in particular) and gained an even greater respect for these native mountaineers who are my people.

Too, after the discovery of the article in the old trunk, I am aware that from Mother, I have been endowed with her ability to put into the written word my thoughts and descriptions of happenings and events. Thus, I have developed my special form of storytelling: oral history transmitted and preserved for this generation and those to come. As a child I had listened to accounts of family "doings", as tales and yarns were told as we sat around the dining table after a meal, or sitting in the warmth of heat of a fireplace, or fixing strawberries, while resting under a shade tree, or while stitching at a quilting bee. The art of storytelling is truly an integral part of my mountain heritage.

The unearthing of the diploma, college newspaper and original speech, and poems written by my mother was the impetus to compile my *Laurel* stories into one volume and to publish my writing of family stories and yarns.

Young Harris College Susan B. Anthony Society, Clyde Arrendale is 2nd from left

# More Treasures

Other treasures from the trunk have been located. A small baby book, with a cover of pink silk decorated with painted rose buds, gives an account of my earliest years. Beginning with my arrival on Sunday, November 18, 1930, memorable events are recorded dating up to my third birthday party.

I remembered that tucked inside the baby book were several sheets of hand-written poems, basically written about me as a toddler between years of 1930 - 1933. This original poetry gives insight and understanding of the interests, values, and thoughts of Mama.

After the birth and loss of her first son, John Patrick, who died at birth, Mama never again penned poetry. Sometimes such a traumatic event results in "closing the door" to such talent as hers. This collection of poems is now being published for the first time in this book.

Following the final poem, entitled "Mother", there are two tributes which were read at the funeral service for Mama on August 23, 1999, at the Tiger United Methodist Church. The first is an eulogy, in poetic prose, composed by family members. The second is a poem written by our friend, Shannon Alley. These comforting words, shared with others, made the loss of our beloved mother more bearable.

---

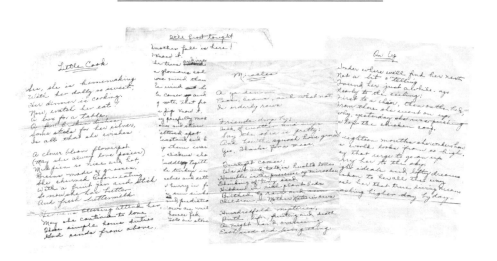

## It'll Frost Tonight

Another Fall is here!
I know it.
The trees and vines are in glorious colors
More vivid than man can paint.
The wind howls around the corner
And hisses a warning note.
Frost will come tonight.
The pigs know it,
They carefully make their beds of leaves and straw
In the most sheltered spot.
Then stand and beg for supper
To keep them warm tonight.
The chickens show it.
They huddle together on their roosts
While the turkeys in the trees shake themselves
And settle to the breeze.
Boys hurry in from the fields as the sun sinks low
Singing and predicting a right early snow!
The cows are milked, the horses fed
All tools are stored within the shed.
After supper a roaring fire is built
That seems to warn each one to get another quilt,
For it will frost tonight!

Clyde A. Pleasants

## On Up

Wonder where we'll find her next?
Not a bit o'telling.
Found her just awhile ago
Nearly to the ceiling!
First to a chair, then on the bed,
From there she went on up.
Why, yesterday she was perching
On top the chicken coop!

At eighteen months she wonders how
The world looks from so high.
May that urge to go on up
Carry her to the sky.
High ideals and lofty dreams
Beckon to her all the way.
Teach her that true living means
Reaching higher day by day.

Clyde A. Pleasants

Riches

She was so tired, nestled in Granny's lap
Sweet eyelids stuck -
Hope she has a  good nap.

There are her toys
Scattered all over the floor -
A string of spools,
There's that old patent leather belt,
An old spice can to rattle
And a discarded clothespin.

And under her little chair,
A kitty.
How those dimpled legs do move
When "It" comes around.
Just let her do him any way,
Sling him by the tail,
Tousle him
And firmer friends never were.

Spools, a belt, a can, a clothespin and a cat.
What better toys for a ten-month old brat?

Clyde A. Pleasants

# Little Cook

See, she is homemaking
With her doll, so sweet,
Her dinner is cooking.
Now, watch her eat!
A box for a table,
A few broken dishes,
Some sticks for her silver,
Is all that she wishes.

A clover bloom flowerpot
(May she always love posies)
Mud pies so nice and hot,
Greens made of grasses.
She churned before eating
With a fruit jar and stick,
So now she has butter
And fresh buttermilk.

Heaven's blessings attend her,
May she continue to love
Those simple home duties
God sends from above.

Clyde A. Pleasants

# Untitled

The clothes hang,
Sweet and clean
Upon the line,
Sunshine purifying.

They were dirty
Jack slid on a red hill.
And that mischievous Gertie,
The tomboy at school.

Maybe the baby
Should have stayed inside
But that yard was so grassy and wondrously wide!

Fishing that afternoon
Did Daddy more good than a trip.
He fished and sang, even went in for a dip.
Yes, I too went out
And made flower beds all day.
Isn't it fun to work in gardens?
It makes me feel such joy.

Even if I am tired
Work is a joy if there is freedom for play.
Life is so full when making a house.

Clyde A. Pleasants

# Miracles

A garden -
Peas, beans, and what not
In orderly rows.

Friends drop by;
Talk of weather and crops.
Say, the okra is pretty
And how the squash have grown!
Yes, thanks for a mess.

Twilight comes;
We sit and talk in hushed tones,
Humble in the presence of miracles.
Thinking of tiny seeds
Hidden in rich plant beds
Birthed by rain and sun
Children - Mother Nature's own.

Hundredfold mysteries,
Birth, life, fruiting and death.
A mighty hand overseeing
Each seed and living thing.

Clyde A. Pleasants

# Mother

Out of this great wide world
There's only one who is always true.
There's one who dreams and works and toils
And thinks always of you.

Her hair may be snowy white
Or black as a raven's wing.
But whenever she thinks of her boy or girl
It makes her dear heart sing.

Perhaps you've gone astray,
The world may turn away.
But your mother waits with outstretched arms
To shelter you from the fray.

Or if you have won fame,
Or honor or wealth or praise,
Your mother is happy and you've
Gladdened her last sweet days.

She cared for you when a babe
She kissed you and made you well,
She listened to all your woes and cares
And lifted you when you fell.

She worried when you were bad
She was glad when you were good
She stayed awake and waited your return
And knew your every mood.

So sing a song of Thanksgiving
For this gift of God so Great.
Live as she taught and when life ends,
You will have nothing to berate!

Clyde A. Pleasants

Clyde A. Pleasants with a young Janie P. in 1931

## MaClyde's Legacy

Today is a very special day. We have gathered here to remember and celebrate the life of Clyde Ellen Arrendale Pleasants English. It is fitting that we be in this particular place to reflect on the good, long life she lived.

When we think of MaClyde, as she was so affectionately known, the word "love" immediately comes to mind, for she deeply loved her family, her church, her friends, and her community.

MaClyde was a wise, wonderfully gifted teacher, and she has taught us well. She inspired us to appreciate and enjoy the little things in life -- beautiful flowers, "family feeds", a good book, crossword puzzles, quilting, nail polish -- in a pretty shade of pink, trips to Rich's Department store, snowflakes, trees -- all trees, the Braves games, the Appalachian Mountains, new babies, a crackling fire, busy hands, coffee, a front porch swing, baby chicks and, of course, chocolate. MaClyde died the way she lived -- with dignity and graciousness. She had that unique ability to make people feel welcome, cared for, and significant. She was a role model, a guide, an encourager, a survivor.

MaClyde's steadfast faith in God sustained her throughout her life just as it blesses us now. I think she would have us remember that we were not created to live on this earth forever, but rather to live in heaven for eternity with God. She would have us comfort one another as we have done and will continue to do. She would remind us that grieving is a natural, healthy process. Each of us must grieve, in our own way, and then we must move forward and seek to live each day to the fullest, just as she did.

We have wonderful memories to cherish. MaClyde's legacy of love, faith, and family will continue to live on in our hearts and minds and will be passed down to the generations that follow. Her love will always be with us. Our cups runneth over. We are truly blessed.

When I was thinking about a verse in the Bible that represented MaClyde, Philippians 4:8-9 came to mind:

"Finally, brothers, whatever is true, whatever is noble, whatever is right, whatever is pure, whatever is lovely, whatever is admirable -- if anything is excellent or praiseworthy -- think about such things. Whatever you have learned or received or heard from me, or seen in me -- put it into practice. And the God of peace will be with you."

Let us pray:

Dear Lord, Our Heavenly Father,

Thank you for all the many blessings you give us each and every day. Thank you for MaClyde and for allowing her so many wonderful years among us. Be with our family as we mourn and give us strength to celebrate her life and what she represented. Lead, guide and protect us. In Christ's name we pray, Amen.

Becky W. Ray and Wesley L. Taylor

---

Mama Clyde had many interests. A favorite was quilting with friends in her beloved home.

Clyde Ellen Arrendale Pleasants English
February 11, 1908 - August 21, 1999

A woman left us today
A woman so elegant and kind
A genteel lady strong in spirit.
A legend in her time...

A sister left us today.
A sister we could talk to and laugh with
As we strolled  down memory lane
A sister who shared times of joy or pain...

A mother left us today.
A mother who cherished every moment of motherhood.
She loved each one unconditionally and as needed
For each one, she understood...

A grandmother and great grandmother left us today.
A grandmother who loved all children regardless of size
Instilling in them their uniqueness
By the twinkle of pride in her eyes...

A wife left us today.
A devoted wife who gave more than her equal part
From an abundance of selfless love
Deep within her heart...

An aunt and cousin left us today.
One who filled a void from the loss we have known
Sharing with us a haven
By making her home our home...

A teacher and volunteer left us today.
A school teacher, a teacher of Sunday School.
Of God. love. life...she understood
That in the very least of us is something good...

A friend and neighbor left us today.
A delightful hostess of quilting bees, tea parties
And her stories of the past
Her touch on our lives will forever last...

But, a woman was born today.
Her childlike smile is even brighter
Her joy incomprehensible
There is no pain, no tears.
Embraced by God through endless years!

*Shannon Alley*

# Chapter 2
# The Early Years

# The Early Years

My very first memory is that of seeing the starlit sky on a clear, cold night, as I was being carried "piggy-back" on my Daddy's shoulders, very secure as I clutched his hands. Mama was beside us as we walked up the school driveway to a PTA meeting. (Isn't this a very appropriate memory, as I have spent much of my life in a schoolhouse!) As I looked upward and marveled at the heavens above, I vividly recall Mama repeating the nursery rhyme: "Twinkle, Twinkle, Little Star / How I wonder what you are? / Up above the world so high. / Like a diamond in the sky".

When I was two years old, I was given a puppy, a purebred collie, who was named Jip. He was identical in size, color, and expressive eyes to Lassie, of movie and TV fame. Jip was a loyal member of our household until he peacefully died on our front porch when I was in the ninth grade. My love of dogs has continued, but I still get teary-eyed and the sniffles whenever I enjoy a "Lassie Come Home" movie.

James Virgil (Jim) Pleasants

Not only do I recall the birth and death of my infant brother, John Patrick, when I was three, but I also vividly remember the joy and excitement with the arrival of my brother, James Virgil, when I was six years old. Three years later my sister, Margaret (Peggy), was born, a sister I had been longing for and a real-life baby doll!

........................................................

Then there were my two personal Roller-Coaster type rides! One concerned the 1928 Chevrolet which was parked near the walnut tree at the bottom of the rock steps at Mama's house. When Daddy and I loaded up for a trip to town, lo and behold, the engine did not start! So Daddy decided to get out of the car (after putting it out of gear) and give it a gentle push down hill.

But the vehicle became a runaway car with me in the passenger seat! Gathering up speed, the car rolled faster and faster down the sloping driveway. I remember seeing the mailbox as the car and I crossed the highway. (Luckily, there was no oncoming traffic.) The car and I jumped over a ditch, and finally came to a stop at the creek in what is now a blueberry patch. I heard Mama on the porch, screaming, "STOP, STOP!" and I saw Daddy dashing as fast as he could after the runaway car and me. I opened the door, got out and to the relief of one and all, I hollered, as loud as I could, "I ain't dead! I ain't dead!" The car had

My father, Miles Otis Pleasants with the 1928 Chevy

a few scratches and dents, but I was alive and well, and none the worse for wear.

My second Roller-Coaster type ride involved my "best buddy" and first cousin, Joanne Ezzard, who was given a "hand-me-down" youth bicycle, green in color. At age five, Joanne was very coordinated. She learned to ride immediately, and the training wheels were removed. Although I was eight years old, it was a very difficult task for me to learn to ride that bike. Finally, I was able to balance, and with Joanne supporting the bike, I, too, would ride back-and-forth on the level farm road by the chicken houses. Being very confident

Joanne Ezzard and Janie Pleasants

now, Joanne and I decided to travel past this area and ride down to the pump station, where there were huge cement vats of poison being prepared to spray the apple orchard. Being the oldest, I was to be first. So with Joanne trotting beside me, I rode down the farm road. As we approached the "Little Orchard", the farm road became very steep. The bicycle and I started downhill, and we traveled faster and faster. No one had ever told me that the bicycle had brakes -- so I gained more momentum. Joanne was running behind me screaming, "Whoa, Whoa!", as I clutched the hand bars

Granddaddy John Arrendale

tightly. Then, the "flying machine and I" bounded directly into the side of the huge cement vat filled with arsenic apple orchard spray, right dab in the middle of the farm crew, the spraying equipment and Granddaddy Arrendale. At first the hands were shocked and speechless, but Granddaddy said as he picked me up, "Dern Grandyongun! Are you hurt?" Luckily, I said, "No, Sir." To which he replied, "You two pick up the pieces of this bicycle and go on back to the house NOW and stay away from the pump station." (I'm sure he had nightmares of what if I had flipped upwards and fallen into the vat of deadly, blue poison. Oh! Me!) I had now survived my second Roller-Coaster type ride and one can understand why I never visit a carnival or go near an amusement park. I've been there, done that, and I have the tee-shirt!

................................................................

There are bittersweet recollections, too. When my Uncle Bumps (John Arrendale, Jr.) had his first payday from his first job after graduating from college, he purchased for me, his only niece, a

Gwen and John Arrendale, Jr. (Uncle Bumps)

miniature tea set. Perfectly arranged in a thin cardboard box, the sixteen piece set was made of reddish-yellow translucent porcelain with a metallic blue border, and decorated with tiny white blossoms. Truly it was a "Made in China" gift. After opening this surprise, I was so excited that I tripped and tumbled off the front porch to the ground below. My China tea set was shattered, and I was heart-broken! As Mama consoled me, she recovered the tea pot, one cup, and one saucer. (These pieces remained on the top shelf of the walnut cupboard until I recently gave them to a granddaughter.) A replacement for the china tea set was never mentioned as the year was 1933, and we were in the midst of The Great Depression.

..............................................................................

Like our Scots-Irish ancestors, Mama taught us to be very frugal, or to be saving, economical, and thrifty. I was well aware of the old sayings: "Waste not, want not" and "It's not how much you earn, but how you manage what you earn". Mama was also a staunch believer in tithing, or giving a tenth of earnings to support the clergy and church. As a member of the Tiger United Methodist Church for most of her lifespan of 91 years, many of her beliefs were Puritanical in origin. She insisted that Sunday should be a day of church activities, rest and renewal. The only "corporal punishment" I ever received at the hands of my mother was an old-fashioned "switching" for disobedience and breaking the Sabbath. I had slipped off with my girl friends to a ball game at the Tiger field on a Sunday afternoon. It was many a day before I even thought about a baseball game, let alone on Sunday!!

.................................................................................

As clear as yesterday, I remember the day of December 7, 1941. Having been out for a drive on a cloudy Sunday afternoon, we stopped at the local "filling station" for ice cream. There we heard the news of a sneak Japanese attack on Pearl Harbor. Hearing this, Mama and Daddy had very worried and concerned looks on their faces. The next day, President Franklin Delano Roosevelt issued a proclamation and World War II began for the United States. For four years (from my age eleven to age 14) the war effort continued. There was rationing of items such as gasoline, sugar and rubber products. With great anxiety, I saw three uncles march off to fight in unheard of places on the globe. I knew, also, the sadness when a cousin was a casualty at the Battle of the Bulge. During this time, there was much speculation concerning the "secret" massive construction project up near Fontana, North Carolina, as many family and neighbors were employed there. Later

Uncle Joel Arrendale
in his WWII dress uniform

I learned this was the building of Oak Ridge, Tennessee, where the first atomic bomb was developed, and which helped end the World War II conflict.

Much to my delight, I received a gift from Aunt Catherine Arrendale, who was a nurse at a military hospital in New Jersey. Inside the package was a matching set of undergarments: a full slip and panties (which were secured by a button on each side, as rubber elastic was unavailable). These items were made of nylon, the first

Aunt Catherine Arrendale

man-made material; they were snow white in color, soft in texture, dried quickly, and I think I was the first young lady in Rabun County to have nylon underwear!

The death of President Roosevelt, who had served three terms in office, came as a shock, and this nation grieved. I sat and listened on the radio as the procession of the funeral train traveled from Warm Springs, Georgia to Washington, DC. Eventually, Mama purchased a television set (black-and-white) and I marveled at this new type of communication.

........................................................................

Recollections are very clear of Mama teaching us three children to appreciate the traditional handicrafts and native art work of this mountainous area. The six foot tall solid walnut cabinet, with four doors, is an excellent example of woodworking. Superbly well constructed by a Smith relative, Mama purchased this piece in the early 1930's. Much "elbow grease" was expended to reveal the beauty of this classic piece of furniture which still stands in the main room of Mama's house.

A pastime of the menfolks was whittling, or the carving of a small piece of wood using a pocket knife. I am always amazed at their creative ability as seen in miniature deer, bears, snakes and sling-shots!

Knitting, crocheting, embroidery of many types and rug making were learned as soon as I could hold a needle! I remember being taught to piece a quilt top either by hand or by pedaling the treadle-type Singer sewing machine. When the poultry industry became big business in this northeast Georgia area, the chicken feed sacks, being very colorful and made of 100% cotton material, were used in many ways by Mama and the womenfolk. I recall wearing "sack" dresses, and many household items were made for the home -- sheets, pillowcases, curtains -- but, most especially, for making quilts. Quilts were a necessity for warmth during the cold winters. White flour sacks and other types had long been put to use by Mama, too.

A spinning wheel and a weaving loom were part of the furnishings at home, and I was well aware of their importance in years gone by. I was not familiar with a potter's wheel, but we cousins were "into" pottery at a very young age! During the warm months of the year, we would play in the creek below the house and dig out the pipe clay. We would mold and make "playhouse" bowls and dishes which were dried in the sun. As an adult I learned that there was a small vein of this special clay that extended from Franklin, North Carolina, to Dahlonega, Georgia, and our creek banks were in a direct line! It was not kaolin, but a fine type of clay used to make the Haviland china in England. The early settlers needed pottery jugs, churns and pots for everyday use and, thus, the earthenware business developed in this area long ago.

Mama taught me the art of earth pigment painting, which is using assorted types and colors of "dirt" to produce an abstract picture or landscape.

Even though I had much "hands on" instruction for daily living, formal schooling was of much importance to our family. I started to school at the old white schoolhouse in Tiger. As there were no school buses at that time, I walked to school daily and when it was raining I wore my pretty red raincoat and hat. There was not a hot lunch food program then, nor indoor toilet facilities. However, improvements came and the Tiger school is still in use today.

John Ezzard milking the cow.
Schooling was very important, but we still had daily chores to be done before and after .

In my childhood, we played various kinds of ball games. We had pastures, creeks and woods available for building forts, camping out sites and had fun in the sun. Next is an account of why I enjoy the game of football so much.

A teacher of agriculture and a distinguished graduate of North Carolina State at Raleigh, North Carolina, my father, Miles Otis Pleasants, was an enthusiastic fan of the college football team. As a young girl, I listened with him to the football games from the table radio every Saturday afternoon during the fall season. From him, I learned the terminology and knowledge of this my favorite sport. When I was "no bigger than a minute", I remember singing the Alma Mater of NC State and doing the "Wolf Pack" cheers!

Having been in failing health for several years, my father suffered a fatal stroke at age 50. (To me, the six-letter word "STROKE" is the most dreaded word in the English language because of its debilitating effect on the human body.)

Miles Otis Pleasants

Mama was left a young widow, and it became even more important that we three siblings continue with our schooling. We all graduated from high school and college with advanced degrees.

———————————————————

Mama Clyde and Janie P. at her graduation from West Georgia College

Dr. Margaret P. Thrasher receiving her Ph.D. degree in Education, 1987

# Seasons of Tiger Mountain

# The Tiger Tale, or How Tiger Got its Name

In the 1700's, the British fought the French for possession of the territory of India. While in this distant land, the British soldiers became used to, and familiar with, the cry and scream of the Bengal tiger, a powerful animal of the Indian jungle. When these same soldiers returned to England after the victorious war, many of them migrated to the New World. With their families, they settled in this northeast corner of Georgia.

Imagine their surprise and shock to hear echoing from the cliffs of a nearby mountain, a piercing cry, like the dying scream of a woman. These were the same sounds they heard in India made by the black striped tiger. Because of these remembered sounds and recurring memories of faraway India, these early settlers called the mountain "Tiger".

The weird, frightening cry was, of course, not made by a tiger but were made by a native mountain cat, a panther, which is commonly called a "painter". Today, the sleek "painter" no longer roams this mountain, for as civilization crept in, it slowly withdrew to more isolated areas located in the higher mountain elevations. Nevertheless, the mountain is still called Tiger Mountain and the neighboring settlement is now the incorporated town of Tiger.

---

# Chapter 3
## Winter

# The Real Story of Big John
## "Big John" and the Biggest, Ugliest, Meanest Bulldog

For sixty years this happening has been told and re-told. Eventually, this event became folklore and "Big John" is known as a folk hero. As recalled, here are the facts. At the end of World War II, "Big John" returned home after serving with the US Marines in the North Pacific theater. He was beginning to adjust to civilian life.

After the square dance on Saturday night, friends gathered at Claude's Cafe in downtown Clayton. The cold north wind was "spitting snow" as it blew off of Black Rock Mountain. As the midnight hour approached, the locals became louder and more boisterous with the sipping of "shine" from coffee mugs. The Clayton Police Chief became concerned about the behavior of the crowd, so he decided to "make an example" of "Big John".

The Chief grabbed him by the arm and proceeded to march him to the nearby jailhouse for booking. Without hesitation, "Big John" slipped out of the heavy coat and darted, with amazing speed, around the corner. The Chief was left holding only the coat. "Big John" had escaped the clutches of the Law - much to the delight and excitement of the onlookers who shouted, clapped, whistled, and cheered.

The Police Chief was greatly aggravated at the loss of the suspect and responded by shooting his .45 pistol up into the air. "Big John", having just survived enemy fire for 87 days on Okinawa was terrified and traveled so fast that he literally ran out of his new black loafers leaving the shoes in the street. Desperately searching for the safety of a foxhole or any secure place, "Big John" dived into the sloping crawl space of the nearby parsonage, the home of the Methodist minister and his family. But the 6 foot tall 180-pound combat veteran was not alone! He had landed on the sleeping biggest, ugliest, meanest bulldog in the county.

The bulldog was so startled and frightened by this intruder, he began scrambling to get out and away. As the floor joists, supported by brick pillars, became gradually closer to the ground and the crawl space narrowed, the bulldog would bump, bump and howl; bump and yelp; bump, bump and bark. This continued until the bulldog was able to make his escape by squeezing out by the front steps.

41

Howling loudly, the bulldog fled the scene, running towards Main Street. Now the Chief assumed that the bulldog was chasing "Big John". Other law officers joined the race. All the while, "Big John" was huddled, warm and safe, under the floor of the preacher's house, watching the "Keystone Cops" in action.

Soon they decided that "Big John" could not be located and gave up the search. Within the hour, a brother and his buddy rescued the black loafers and the winter coat. Gently tooting the car horn and driving very slowly, the two circled the area until "Big John" quickly and quietly emerged from the hiding place and home he went! "Big John" had made BUSH BOND one more time; and at last account, the biggest, ugliest, meanest bulldog was seen traveling on the road to seek safer refuge elsewhere, past Tiger Mountain on south to Athens town. It has been reported that the biggest, ugliest, meanest bulldog became the earliest UGA mascot for the football team at Georgia.

# A Bad Hair Day Made Good

My son, Wesley, his wife, Karen, his mother-in-law, Darlene, and I made preparations for a vacation trip to New England. We carefully packed essential clothes and necessities, including "a mess of green beans" for my cousin, Joanne, in Maine. Of course, for the occasion I had a new haircut, style, and perm before we left.

Our journey north began. While we were visiting a historic lighthouse, a dense fog rolled in and my hair became very frizzy. After enjoying a lobster boil in the bright sunlight, with a sea breeze blowing, my hair locks became very dry and dull. Caught in a Nor'easter, which drenched me and my hair, it was obvious that a conditioner was needed. Enjoying the beach and swimming in the salt water contributed to the deterioration of my tousled, damaged hair. Alas, I was a mess!

On Friday morning of that week, we four motored down to New York to attend the wedding and festivities of my nephew, Paul, and his lovely bride, De Anna. Upon checking into the Saratoga Springs Inn, I inquired of the clerk as to where a beauty shop was located, so I could get a "do", and look presentable for the rehearsal dinner that evening. The clerk sent me over two blocks and, upon opening the door, I saw that the beauty salon was busy with the regular Friday customers. Every dryer was occupied by little old ladies! I waited at the desk; and, eventually, an operator came over. Then, I simply asked, in a polite and friendly manner, if there was an available appointment for a shampoo and set. Looking at me, she replied in a haughty accent, "We are not magicians. We are beauticians!"

Reacting to such a sarcastic comment, I was speechless! Immediately the owner-manager appeared and to "mend the fence" she stated that at 4:30 p.m. she could personally do my hair, but only a wash and blow-dry. Upon arriving at the beauty parlor later, the owner-manager began shampooing my hair. Just to make conversation, she asked me where I lived. When I told her that my home was a small town halfway between Atlanta, Georgia and Asheville, North Carolina, with the name of Tiger, she suddenly stopped in amazement. She declared that she had just returned from a week in Rabun County looking for real estate investments.

As we continued to talk, I received the works: a shampoo, a moisturizing hot oil treatment, a set, and a comb out! Furthermore, the owner-manager offered to check my hair prior to the wedding the next day!

The photographs of the happy event reveal that my hair was truly silky, shiny with not a strand out of place. Who said that a beautician is not a magician?

# MO-THER Tales: part deux

Ordinarily, my four children refer to me as "Mama", or "Mom", or even "Janie P.". But in times of stress, I am called "MO-THER".

On a cool evening, I answered the telephone to hear second daughter Rebecca calling. "MO-THER! MO-THER!" I quickly sensed a problem. In a low whisper, she pleaded, "MO-THER, I have been locked inside my car, for 45 minutes now, and I can't get out." It being a new vehicle, I found this difficult to understand. I asked her if she had pushed the unlock button and panic buttons, to which she replied, "So much that the computer must be mesmerized." Then I inquired, "Have you called 911 to help?"

"No, MO-THER, I'm too embarrassed! I've waved for help, but all these friendly souls just smile and wave back!"

A long silence, then, "MO-THER, the back left door is slightly open, just stay on the phone and I'm going to try to crawl over into the back seat." I could hear the struggle as she announced that one leg was over, that the other leg was over, and then all of Becky tumbled into the back seat. I heard her open the door and as she walked away from the car she said, " Bye, Mama; I'm fine now."

..............................................................................................

Years ago, daughters three and I were at a miniature street circus and pony show. The oldest one, Judy, who was six-years-old, was petting the animals, especially the ponies, when I heard a cry for help, "MO-THER, MO-THER!!" When I looked around at Judy, her eyes were wide with fright and she was pointing downward at her foot. A hoof of the little horse was on top of Judy's left foot and her little white sandal. The owner of that hoof was gazing at her, face to face! With the help of the attendant, the hoof was removed. Unhurt and with a sigh of relief, she said, "That feels better, Mama. Now I'm ready to play!"

..............................................................................................

Answering the phone, I heard the excited yet desperate voice of youngest daughter Dawne saying, "MO-THER, MO-THER!"

"What is the matter?" I quizzed her.

"MO-THER, while the gas was pumping into my car, I went inside to pay. Then, I drove off without removing the nozzle and hose! Now the whole thing is banging and clanging against my car and the man at the service station is waving, yelling, and running after me"

"Dawne, listen. Go back to the service station, return the gas nozzle and hose, get out your checkbook and pay for any damages and don't worry about any dents!"

Relieved, she said, "Okay, and thanks, Mama!"

When I answered the ring of the telephone on a particular Saturday afternoon, I heard the distressed voice of my son, Wesley. "MO-THER," Mark's son, Ashley, has been killed in a farm machinery accident. What do I say and what shall I do?"

In a state of shock myself, I was able to reply, "Let Mark know that you will be beside him as long as you are needed to help in any and every way - be it to sit quietly to listen, to cry with him, even to recollect the good times"

"But, MO-THER, Ashley was only 25 years old"

"Son, don't try to understand this tragedy now, just hold on so that you all can get through the next difficult days. Remind Mark that our Heavenly Father has promised to sustain us, and give us strength over the long haul."

"Thanks, Mama. I love you."

Janie P.'s children: Dawne W. Bryan, Becky W. Ray,
Wesley L. Taylor, and Judy W. Scott

# The Waddling Bear

A few years ago, we folks here in Rabun endured a most severe winter. Not only were there inches of snowfall, but with subfreezing temperatures, the snow changed to ice. Glacier like conditions resulted! Many of us were without electricity or water, and we were truly home bound.

At last, the highway was scraped and traffic began slowly moving. When I saw the rural mail carrier delivering my mail, I became very determined to overcome the weather conditions, and get over to the mailbox. After all, the weekly local newspaper had just arrived, and I was anxious to read the news on that cold Thursday.

So, I commenced to get dressed to brave the elements. As the north wind was howling off Tiger Mountain, I put on my long black fleece jacket, black warm-up pants, a gray vest, a heavy dark scarf, and my white woolen gloves.

Off I went! I gingerly made my way down the front steps and slowly moved down the hill. Using my walking stick, I gradually made my way along the driveway. Then I arrived at the wooden bridge. Much to my dismay, it was a solid sheet of ice! My only choice was to get down on my hands and knees and crawl to the other side. This I did and then walked upright to the mailbox for the desired letters and paper.

Then I realized that to return back to the house, I would once again have to get down on all-fours and slowly maneuver myself across the slick surfaces of the frozen planks. After completing this feat, I carefully regained my balance and completed my journey to the house. Shedding my dark wraps, I settled down by the warm fire to read the mail.

Soon thereafter, a truck, with blinking yellow lights flashing, drove across the bridge. Behind the "government" vehicle there was a cage-like contraption, a mobile bear trap!

Hearing the noise, Melvin went to the door to investigate. The uniformed man yelled, "Where's the bear?"

To this, Melvin responded, "What bear?" The state employee, with tranquilizer gun in hand, stated, "Our office just received an emergency call from a motorist who was traveling by here and

46

reported that there was a large black bear "waddling" across you bridge!

Melvin was speechless. Then it dawned on him, and he replied, "Oh, that was my wife crawling across the bridge to the mailbox!" Seeing the bear cage on hand, Melvin was inspired and asked, "Could you guys go ahead and load up Janie P. and take her with you? During this cold spell we have been like two old boar cats -- when one moves the other one growls!"

Hastily, the men replied that no such action was in their job description, and off they went, with an empty bear trap dragging behind.

By now, I'm totally devastated! The very idea of using the descriptive word "waddling" to describe me crossing the icy bridge! Anyone of those other terms - creeping along, or moving cautiously, or clumsily rocking from side to side, would have been more suitable.

Within days, a warm rain fell and the snow and ice disappeared. The Spring thaw had arrived! Melvin and the John Deere tractor began moving about, and life returned to normal.

---

# A Valentine Special - "Pummie Day"

If a Valentine party is being planned for February 14th, there is a concoction to serve the guests which will make this a most memorable event. The "makings" of this drink have been passed down from generation to generation of mountain folks. It is called "24-hour cocktail" or the "recipe". The ingredients and directions are provided here.

In a five- gallon churn, pour a 1/2 gallon of moonshine whiskey. Add, 1/2 gallon of spring water. Cut, squeeze, and drop into the churn, two dozen oranges, a dozen lemons, and three grapefruits. Add three cups of sugar. Stir and cover with cheesecloth. Let this sit for 24 hours. Remove the fruit halves and squeeze. To remove the seeds and excess pulp, strain through the cheesecloth into a second five-gallon churn. To serve, pour over ice. Salt generously. (Caution: upon drinking, be aware of the consequences.) And thus the story...

On the day of the Valentine "do- up", and after the 24-hour waiting period, Melvin began to remove the fermented fruit halves from the big churn. Pummie Day had arrived! He squeezed and he squeezed. In order to conserve every drop of the "recipe", it was necessary to lick and slurp the pummies of two dozen oranges (48 halves), the dozen lemons (24 halves) and the three grapefruit (six halves). The remains of the halves, the "pummies", were then tossed over the pasture fence.

Beauty, the milk cow, trotted down the hill to check on the "goings-on", and immediately began eating the pummies. She listened as Melvin sang, loud and clear, "Let me call you sweetheart." After several renditions of this, he began singing the lyrics of "O My Darling Clementine," but to the tune of "Faded Love" by Bob Wells.

As the final step of straining the recipe was completed, the host lost his balance and slid off the back porch onto the soft dirt. Smiling, the host began reciting, "Roses are red, violets are blue, sugar is sweet and so are you...", as he fell asleep on Pummie Day.

Meanwhile, the effects of consuming the discarded pummies became most evident on Beauty the cow. When she heard the call for milking time, Beauty kicked up her heels, leaped from side to side, mooing and bawling as her eyes glared, her tail waved wildly, and her full milk bag flopped from side to side, as she traveled to the barn. (When Mama Clyde reported to me on the next day, that the rich creamy jersey milk from Beauty strangely tasted like eggnog and had a distinct bite to it, I simply did not respond, but read the Valentine's Day card instead).

Later, the guests arrived for the Valentine party. The host was "all cleaned up", and greeted everyone with a glass of the "recipe". When the five-gallon churn was empty of "The 24-hour cocktail", the party goers began to leave. I noted there was a great similarity between the behavior of the intoxicated cow and the guests as they staggered to their cars!

Being a teetotaler, I can only state what I observed on Pummie Day years ago. I do know that I saw a cow who thought she could jump over the moon. Maybe this recipe is a ladies' specialty, for, at daylight the next morning, Beauty the cow was standing at the gate begging for more crushed fruit halves. But, to no avail, for Pummie Day was over!

---

# The Day Atlanta Traffic Stood Still

Years ago, when I was a school principal here in Rabun County, a field trip to Atlanta in January was planned. The elementary students would tour the State Capitol, meet the Governor and State Legislative members, and then attend the three-ring circus! The excitement was great! Permission slips were returned to the classroom teacher; chaperones were selected; a sack lunch was prepared by the lunchroom staff and Mr. "Footsie" O'Neal.

Transportation details were completed and the Big Day arrived. As the boys and girls loaded on to the seven yellow school buses, I noted that the winter sky was very grey, and the temperature was cold. Hours later, the group was seated, and each student was happily watching the three-ring circus. Just before the final act was over, I received a frantic telephone call from the school superintendent, who said, "Get back home as soon as you can! The temperature is fast dropping and snow is forecast." So with haste, the children and adults loaded onto the seven buses which were running with heaters on, for the ride back to the mountains. However, we had a PROBLEM! The school buses could not exit the parking lot due to fast moving traffic; the five way intersection was busy with many cars and trucks. After waiting several minutes, I had a "dern female notion". I ran to bus #1, and shouted, "I'm going to get us on the road. When I wave and point north, move out!" At bus #2, I gave the same instructions -- on to bus #3, bus #4, #5, and #6. Then, to bus #7, I spoke to the driver, "As you pull out, open the door so I can jump on. Don't leave me PLEASE!" With this, I marched myself right out into the Atlanta traffic and stood directly under the stoplight. I stood there, holding up my hand and wearing my most stern "school teacher" look, and the many vehicles screeched to a stop! I then waved bus #1 out of the parking lot. Next bus #2, #3, #4 pulled onto the main street. Just as bus #5 was leaving an Atlanta police car arrived on the scene. With the blue lights flashing, the officer asked, "What are you doing lady?" As I waved bus #6 on its way, I replied "This is an EMERGENCY! These school busses must move out as snow and ice are expected in the mountains!" As the law officer got out of his patrol car, I rushed to get on bus #7 as it exited. We heard the cop yell, "Lady, if you ever need a job, our force can sure use you in traffic control!" Without further stress, the motorcade of yellow buses "got home before dark", and before the snowflakes fell. To this day, I often see a former student who recalls the day "that Miz Taylor stopped the traffic in Atlanta".

# Janie P. and Mr. Law Man

Several years ago, while on my way to a conference in Oakwood, I found myself in the midst of new highway construction for the proposed I-985. The day was extremely cloudy and the new road signs had not been put into place. As I was driving along, I decided that this was certainly a friendly area as all the cars and trucks were honking their horns, waving and blinking their car lights. Suddenly, I realized that I was traveling in the wrong direction on the interstate. Was I going south in the north lanes or was I going north in the south lanes? I did not know, but in order to get out of the predicament, I just began "back-backing up".

Immediately, a patrol car with blue lights flashing appeared. As the uniformed law enforcer approached, he asked, "Lady, what are you doing?" I answered that I was back-backing up. To this he replied, "Please do not say back-backing up. Instead, respond that you are operating this vehicle in reverse!" I replied, "Yes, Ossifer." Then the face of the patrolman became very red, and he stated that I was not to call him "Ossifer" for he was a qualified protector of the motoring public - and what was my problem? "Well, Mr. Law Man, I seem to be lost. I cannot see the sun, because of the clouds, to get my bearing on where is north, south, east or west! You see sir, I'm from *Foxfire* country, and the book says that green moss always grows on the north side of a tree. If I can locate a tree, then I could travel south to my meeting."

Shaking his head and mumbling, he got out the ticket book and asked to see my driver's license. As he checked this legal document, the Law Man asked "Where is Tiger?" "Sir," I exclaimed, "Surely you know that Tiger is a small town half-way between Atlanta and Asheville, North Carolina, and let me tell how Tiger got its name! Here's how..." By now the patrolman was somewhat agitated -- he wasn't sure which was north either! Putting away the ticket book, he said to me, "Lady, can you follow my patrol car, with the blue lights, as we travel south down this road?" To this I nodded my head and stated, "Yes sir, Mr. Law Man." Next, he announced to me that when I had completed my day at the conference, he would be waiting for me at the big intersection, and I was to follow the patrol car NORTH. Furthermore, he was notifying the police department of Lula, Alto, Cornelia, Demorest, Clarkesville, and Tallulah Falls to verify that I was still motoring NORTH, and in the proper lane! As I drove back to Tiger, I waved and tooted my horn at the various "Ossifers" who watched me travel NORTH.

From the west, the setting afternoon sun broke through the cloud layer and shone brightly on Tiger Mountain as I arrived. I was so thankful to know my whereabouts, and that no more "back-backing up" would be necessary!

# Cupid's Arrow Strikes in Hawaii

*Author's Note: To celebrate Valentine's Day on Thursday, February 14th, I am sharing this true account of love and romance involving my brother, Jim Pleasants, who was stationed in Hawaii in the spring of 1959. This story begins:*

It was close to midnight when the pretty brunette entered the all-night diner in Honolulu and considered which of the few vacant stools she should sit on. It had been a long rough flight, and the crew of the Pan Am flight from Wake Island had been busy, so the stewardess hadn't eaten. The young lady was hungry and in no mood to be harassed.

She chose a seat beside a young man with a "high and tight" haircut and then ordered a sandwich. It took forever, but he finally spoke to her.

The conversation started slowly. He was a Marine fighter pilot stationed at Kaneohe Bay MCAS, on the other side of Oahu. His squadron was trying to select a "Miss Crusader," and that he would like to enter her name. He would need a picture and other information. The winner would receive among other prizes, a ride in the supersonic jet.

She agreed to this and promised to call him on her next flight through Honolulu.

She did, and they saw each other several times on her fly-throughs. After several months, he took her to the flight line on the base, where she realized that no one else had ever heard of the "Miss Crusader" contest, and that the Crusader jet had only one seat (the pilot's).

Nevertheless, my sister-in-law Jeanne agreed to marry my brother Jim 48 years ago in Hawaii. Before too long, in a letter to his mother, Jim wrote, " I am going to get married! No definite date... but should be sometime in December. Can you come? Her name is Jeanne and she is from northern Michigan and is now a stewardess from Pan American....real good looking...about 5' 6" or so, dark hair and eyes, very chic. You'll like her, I know." The wedding was set for December 12th, 1959 in Hawaii.

Immediately, Mama Clyde scheduled a substitute teacher for an entire week for her home economics/science classes at Rabun County High School. Then, she bought her airline ticket, packed her "grip" and, with a sense of adventure, off she flew! She had a wonderful trip, and Mama Clyde got acquainted with the bride-to-be as they cleaned and prepared the newlyweds' nest. (During this time, the two were also present at the 17th memorial service of the Japanese attack on Pearl Harbor.)

Mama Clyde was delighted with the marriage of her handsome son and the beautiful daughter-in-law. Disembarking from the airplane at the Atlanta airport, she was happy, exhausted, and wearing a Hawaiian lei!

After Jim completed his tour of duty, the couple returned to the States by way of San Francisco, where Jeanne had been based. Packing up clothes and household goods, they headed east in her 1957 pink and charcoal grey DeSoto. Their destination was Athens, where Jim was enrolled in the School of Law at the University of Georgia.

Our family was pleased that Jim would be back home, and we could hardly wait to meet and welcome Jeanne. She arrived as a stunning beauty with the most gracious of manners and she adjusted well to us in-laws in southern Appalachia. Jeanne had traveled the world from Istanbul to Paris to Hong Kong and all of the exotic places in between -- and now she was here at Tiger Mountain.

Jim and Jeanne have "lived happily ever after" and blessed our family with two children and four grandchildren. I am grateful that in 1959, a certain flight attendant on a Pan Am plane had a layover in Honolulu--and, thus, a Valentines tale for me to tell in 2008!

Jeanne and Jim Pleasants in 2007

# Chapter 4
# Spring

# Home Improvement Tales

*With the arrival of April, the usual cleaning, makeovers, and "sprucing-up" of the house and yard begin. I vividly recall two such occasions!*

One spring-time, years ago, I was informed the Easter Bunny was bringing to me a BIG SURPRISE on Good Friday afternoon. Following a most enjoyable "family feed", I was instructed to remain up at Mama Clyde's house for just one hour; then I would be allowed to see my Easter surprise.

Down the hill at my house, there was much activity. As a pick-up truck backed up to the porch, daughters B. and J. and their spouses, declared that a bathroom remodeling kit had been purchased from a home-builder warehouse. The salesman assured them that any "do-it-yourselfer" could renovate and customize any bathroom anywhere in just one hour!

*Big Melvin, in his easy chair, listens carefully, and mumbles that the Easter Bunny was going to be very busy!*

The four began unloading a tub-surround kit, a new shower door, a vanity with lavatory, and matching towel and toilet paper holders. The new commode, in a box, remained on the truck.

*As he watches, Big Melvin has become very concerned that he has not seen a toolbox or any plumbing equipment with which to complete the SURPRISE. Of even greater concern was the fact that the two sons-in-law had no construction experience and daughters B. and J. even less!*

After locating an old bent screwdriver and a rusty saw, the Helpers of the Easter Bunny began the process of dismantling the bath lavatory. Two hours passed without much progress, but eventually the sink was hauled out the door and discarded -- temporarily!

*Big Melvin, sitting in his recliner, began to wonder, was this an Easter surprise or a Halloween prank?*

Since the new vanity did not fit into the allotted space, the "crew" decided to install the three pre-cut pieces of interior bathroom siding (the tub enclosure set) which were cut square; but unfortunately, due to age and wear, the old bathroom was not square! So nothing fit; things were either too long, too short, or too wide. The Easter

Bunny Helpers were somewhat perturbed at this predicament, but the plan to remove the commode must go forward!

*Big Melvin, leaning back in his easy chair, dozed off to sleep. Awakening, he mumbled, "This nightmare is really happening, will I ever be able to shower or flush again?"*

By now my brother Jim and my cousin Bill had wandered down the hill to view the Easter Surprise. Being two semi-skilled craftsmen, they immediately halted the removal of the commode and replaced the bolts into the floor. Damage control had begun! Next the two began restoring the lavatory to a functioning state.

*Big Melvin covers his ears as much flowery language was heard which will not be quoted here in deference to the gentle, tender ears of the Laurel readers.*

As the sun sank behind Tiger Mountain, the call came for me to return to my home. Amidst the chaos and confusion, daughters B. and J., and their spouses announced that all of the bathroom remodeling materials would be my Easter present, but that I should immediately hire a carpenter and plumber to help the Easter Bunny finish the job. By the next week, skilled workmen had completed the improvements to the bathroom and the labor cost was only a few hundred dollars. This was "well worth the money" for many years of service resulted after the remodeling of the bathroom was completed that spring.

I shall always be grateful to daughters B. and J. for the time, energy, and "cold, hard cash" expended in planning this Easter gift. Their intentions were good and appreciated. They were misled by a "smooth-talking" salesman. Daughters are indeed special!

..........................................................................................

On a warm spring day Big Melvin (known as the Bean Man of Rabun) decided that since there was little or no air movement, it would be an ideal time to spray-paint the outside walls of our house. The green stain would give a new fresh appearance.

The gallons of green stain and the paint sprayers were purchased by the Bean Man. Enlisting the assistance of his brother, Ervin, the two went to work. But, lo-and-behold, the early morning breeze turned into a gusty wind! Soon the coveralls, the faces, the hair and all exposed surfaces were a green color; only the large protective goggles were clear.

As lunchtime approached the two "men in green" went to eat at a nearby tearoom. Both men noticed that the parking lot was filled with cars. When they entered the dining area, the monthly luncheon meeting of the Ladies Society Club was in full session. Imagine the surprise and shock as the "green men" entered! The guest speaker lost her line of thought as all of the women turned to stare. Were the two "men in green" aliens from outer space? Were they foreigners from a distant planet? Had they landed in a flying saucer on Tiger Mountain? In the midst of the total silence, the two "strangers" placed their order. Upon hearing their voices, the club members were relieved to realize that the two were harmless homefolks who were completing a home beautification project.

I've often wondered how the club secretary recorded the minutes of that eventful day. "The guest speaker was interrupted, and the membership startled and amazed with the arrival of two individuals wearing large goggles, dressed in green, who resembled 'space men.' However, the determination was made that the two were local citizens and neighbors who were spraying the exterior of the home with a green stain as a spring cleaning task. The two 'strangers' simply wanted a hot meal in the middle of the day. Since there was no danger of being captured or held hostage, the club meeting continued."

How do I know that Melvin, the "Bean Man" was the "man from Mars" that spring day? When Wesley and I returned home from school that afternoon, the outside of the house looked magnificent! Big Melvin was resting in the easy chair, still covered from head to toe with the green stain - exactly the same green color as the fields of "half-runner" beans growing down by the creek. Spring had Sprung!

---

# Flowers Year Round

Dear readers, the year 2006 has come and gone. Many happenings and events will be remembered by "me and mine" and the various flowers, which have special meaning, will be recalled, also.

January: The north wind did blow and we did have snow. Found under the snowfall and by digging under the decaying leaves, the delicate trailing arbutus was located. A cluster of tiny white-pink blooms were seen amongst the leathery-green leaves of the evergreen plant. The trailing arbutus and the early lavender crocus assured us that springtime was near. Also, on Tiger Mountain, the galax plants hug the ground on the north side. The galax leaves are deep green in color, flat and somewhat heart-shaped. My grandmother, Tallulah Edwards Arrendale, recalled using the galax leaves to form wreaths during the winter months for funeral services. There were no blooming flowers, nor were there florists or garden centers nearby, only galax leaves were available.

February: As the yellow jonquils and the gold-yellow forsythia began to bud, the decision was made to restore, renovate, and make historically livable the old homeplace. (The original log house was built in 1825.) Great care was taken to preserve the shrubs, like the early flowering quince, which is a spring bush with red flowers. The heirloom bulbs in the yard, which had been passed on from generation to generation, were protected. The black walnut trees were not to be disturbed. On Valentine's Day, we recalled the old familiar verse: "Roses are red. Violets are blue. Sugar is sweet--and so are you!"

March: With our Scots-Irish heritage, many of us celebrated St. Patrick's Day on Friday, March 17th, by the wearing of green and displaying the symbol of the shamrock, a clover-like plant with three green leaflets. Here is an Irish blessing to share with you: "May your neighbors respect you, Trouble neglect you, The angels protect you... and Heaven accept you".

April: Sunday, April 16th, was Easter Day, and the "Lily of the Valley" is a most cherished flower in these mountains.The sweet fragrance of these small bell-shaped blooms brought back memories of Easter bonnets and egg hunts over the years. Now the apple trees, pear trees, and other fruit trees are in full bloom. As the spring breeze gently blows, the air is filled with blossoms and the scent of spring.

May: Sure enough, the April showers brought May flowers. The white blossom of the Cherokee rose, the pink color of the climbing rose and the purple, or Dutch, iris were aglow. Mother's Day was celebrated on Sunday, May 14th. Mothers were remembered in the traditional manner: a red rose was worn on the lapel if the mother is alive; a white rose worn if the mother is no longer with us, but has received her Heavenly reward.

June: During this season, the mountain laurel (also called ivy) was in full bloom. This evergreen shrub with pink flowers and shiny leaves is a favorite! By Father's Day, the daylilies, in an array of colors, were seen along the roadsides and in the gardens and fields. The hydrangea is a plant beloved by my family members, with the bluish or pink or purple large blooms, and is a delightful source for use in decorating for weddings, showers, and "do-ups".

July: The Fourth of July was celebrated on a Tuesday this past year. The red geranium, the white "glads" and the blue of cornflower (or bachelor button) remind us of the colors of the flag, as does an Independence Day red, white and blue dessert of a strawberry-blueberry shortcake with white whipped cream. And we all joined in singing "God Bless America".

August: The Tiger lily, with its bloom of bright orange flowers with tiny black spots, could be seen by the steps of Mama's house located at the base of Tiger Mountain. In a nearby garden, there were dahlias which bloomed in many differing colors with some blossoms being up to ten inches in width. The sheer size and bright colors of the dahlias made this a favorite of the local mountain people. On the porch, the hanging baskets were filled with impatiens in many beautiful colors.

September: The school bells rang once again with the jingle "Reading, writing and arithmetic; computers, iPods and meter sticks". As the school buses rolled by, the mountain countryside was bright with the yellow goldenrod, the purple asters, and the colorful chrysanthemums. In earlier times, all members of a pioneer family worked together to gather the crops before frost and winter arrived. One old saying, to speed up the process of harvesting, was "Just load the wagon! Don't worry about the old blind mule. It will go straight to the barn".

October: The leaf season has arrived! The red maple and the yellow poplar trees are radiant, and the mountains are spectacular in their brilliant fall foliage. I recall this poem: "Come, said the Wind to the Leaves one day. Come o'er the meadows and we will play! Put on your dress of scarlet and gold; for summer is gone and the days are cold".

November: Veterans' Day was commemorated on Saturday, November 11th with flags, speeches, songs, and red poppy flowers. These verses were remembered: "In Flanders fields the poppies blow, between the crosses, row on row...". The lovely Thanksgiving/ Christmas cacti were beginning to bloom, and the feast of "turkey and all the fixings" was enjoyed, after we had traveled "over the river and through the woods to Grandmother's house we go...". Each of us was truly thankful for this season of faith, hope, and love.

December: Early in this month the red berries on the holly tree and the deeper reds of the nandina bush indicated that Christmas time was on the way! Christmas here in Rabun land was a wondrous time as we shared the pleasure of the season with family and friends. On December 26th, the twelve Ruling Days arrived, running through the Twelfth Night on January 7th, 2007. By keeping a daily weather account for these twelve calendar days, the "old-timers" stated that a forecast for the next twelve months could be predicted. For example, if the fourth Ruling Day (December 29th) is foggy and rainy one can expect the fourth month, April, to have similar conditions.

May happiness, like the beauty of the flowers, surround you in the upcoming year. Special wishes for a blessed New Year.

---

# The Janie P. Quilt

Several years ago a Foxfire staff member contacted my mother, Clyde, and asked her to please schedule a quilting bee in her "old timey house" in Tiger. The British Broadcasting Company (BBC) was due to arrive soon to document the educational program of Foxfire, and the BBC crew was most interested in filming an authentic quilting party.

Mama Clyde readily agreed and began making plans for this "do-up". The decision was made that the quilt top would be pieced in the heritage "log cabin" pattern. Furthermore, the finished product would be given to me - a quilt for Janie P.!!

On the following Tuesday, the BBC technicians appeared and immediately began covering the walls and ceiling with a special material to control the amount of light in the large front room. Due to the age of Mama Clyde's house, all electrical circuits were tested for safety. The cameras and other equipment were put in place. The handmade wooden quilting frame was suspended from the ceiling, with straight chairs placed on each side. The quilt lining, the cotton batting and the top were "put in" the frame. As the quilters from the Tiger Mountain area arrived with thimbles, needles, and spools of thread, they sat down and went to work.

Eventually the director from the BBC stated that when he said, "Roll cameras," he expected total silence from the Foxfire students, staff, and crew. However, the quilters were to continue working and to "act natural". As the cameras rolled, one little lady on the far side inquired, "Clyde, honey, does your roof leak?"

"No! My roof does not leak! Why do you ask?" replied my mother, who was a little put out by the question.

"Clyde, honey, there is a wet spot about the size of a saucer on this quilt," commented the lady. All the quilters now quietly pondered this statement with a few, "Ohs!" and "Ahs!"

"Clyde, honey, you got a cat?" questioned another quilting lady.

"Yes, I've got cats and the cutest yellow kitten you have ever seen! In fact, it was sleeping on this quilt when I got up this morning."

Again, there was a busy silence as the quilters pondered this last comment and continued to act natural. Then...

"Clyde, honey, you know what? That cat has peed on this quilt!" None of the quilters reacted and continued to busily quilt. The director, on the other hand, began laughing so hard that he fell from his chair and rolled under the quilt. He laughed so much that he had to be helped back to his chair. He gained his composure and said, "Roll cameras, again!"

Then another quilter calmly suggested, "Clyde honey, just rub a little of Clorox on the spot, and it won't have a scent nor stain."

It was here that I spoke up because I could not bear to have bleach used on my beautiful "Log Cabin" quilt for whatever reason, and so this is how my quilt got its special name, "The Janie Pee Quilt".

Her hands never idle,
Janie P. has inherited her
mother's love for quilting.
Janie P. combines
two of her passions:
storytelling and quilting.

# The Doctor, the Lady Teacher and the Bean Man of Rabun

The paths of these three crossed on a sunny day in June of 1963. First, Dr. Ed Angel was a compassionate family physician, a skilled surgeon, a wise businessman and a native of Macon County, North Carolina. He and his brother, Dr. Furman Angel, established a private hospital in Franklin, which was the only medical center in this mountainous region.

Second, Miss Gladys Shirley was a beloved school teacher now retired from the Rabun County system. She was a kind and dedicated teacher. This I know for I was a student in her second and third grade classrooms. She had a most positive influence on each of us who studied and learned in her classroom.

Finally, Melvin Taylor, my husband, was known as the "Bean Man". A truck farmer for over 50 years, he has produced thousands of bushels of beans, corn, and other garden vegetables. Born and raised in Rabun County, Melvin survived the Great Depression and the battles of World War II. He is an example of America's greatest generation.

After being discharged from service, Melvin became an active blood donor. He has O-negative type blood, which can blend with all other blood types, and he gave blood generously to save Rh babies, wreck victims, and other medical emergencies as needed.

And now the story:

At about noon on that warm spring day, the telephone rang. When I answered, the voice said, "I've got to get in touch with Melvin at once! Where is he?" To this, I replied, "He is cultivating beans in the field down by Tiger Creek." Then, the voice said, "This is Ed Angel at the Franklin Hospital. Tell him I need a blood transfusion for a critically-ill surgical patient, whose blood pressure is fast dropping. Tell him not to take time to wash up, nor stop for coffee in town and hurry!"

So I dashed to the field and delivered the message. Melvin stopped the John Deere tractor, jumped into his truck to travel the 22 miles north to Franklin. Unknown to either of us was that the patient was Miss Gladys Shirley who was barely clinging to life.

As Melvin arrived at the hospital, the orderlies met him at the door, placed him on a gurney, covered the work boots, dusty jeans and sweaty shirt with a sterile green sheet, pushed him into the operating room directly next to the surgical bed. By tube, the donor and the patient were connected and the new supply of blood was pumped directly from vein of the donor into the vein of the patient. Dr. Angel, the operating room staff, and Melvin watched as the blood pressure began to rise and the vital signs of Miss Gladys became more normal. Eventually, Dr. Angel gave Melvin the high sign; he was rolled out and back home to farming he went.

But this story is not ended. Dr. Ed Angel vowed and declared that as Miss Gladys slowly regained consciousness after the anesthetic, she was heard softly mumbling "B-e-a-n-s" and then "C-o-r-n". Next, she kept repeating "half-runners" and "Silver Queen corn". Finally, just before awakening, Miss Gladys was saying, "Picking green beans and a-peddling sweet corn." The rich red blood had done its work!

What began as an ordinary day became *extra-ordinary*. The Doctor did not lose the patient; the Teacher completely recovered from this traumatic surgery; and the Bean Man had once again, without hesitation, provided life-saving blood for a friend and neighbor.

Melvin Taylor, the Bean Man, with son Wesley

# A Singing to Remember

One a warm summer evening, years ago, the melodious sounds of gospel music and hymns being sung could be heard echoing from the rock cliffs, the ridges, and the hollows of Tiger Mountain. From whence cometh this majestic music? A movie crew from Atlanta and Hollywood arrived in Rabun County to film a movie entitled "There's a Still on the Hill". The year was 1966. The featured singer-actress was the talented and popular Dottie West. She had the vivacious personality of a red-head, lively and spirited. Scenes to be filmed included an old-fashioned church song service and a typical Sunday School picnic of the 1920's era. Permission was granted to use the building and grounds of the historic Tiger United Methodist Church (which was constructed in 1897) for the filming of these events. At the scheduled time, members of the church and community arrived dressed in costumes and outfits previously worn in the annual Mountaineer Festival.

With the filming of the picnic, the "extras" became familiar with the instructions given by the director and crew; and each found Dottie West to be friendly and charming. Next, the congregation gathered inside the church and was seated on the handhewn pine pews. One of the musical crew was seated at the antique pump organ (which was purchased to provide music for a revival in 1898); and another musician began striking chords on the upright piano (which was given to the church by the Dr. and Mrs. J.C. Dover). The professionals began playing and Dottie began singing the beloved gospel song, "I'll Fly Away". It was a magnificent performance! Then with a wave of her hand, Dottie informed the director and the movie crew that she wanted to keep on singing -- and she did! Hymns such as "The Old Rugged Cross", "Amazing Grace", "Sweet Hour of Prayer", "Precious Memories", "When We All Get to Heaven", and "Go Tell it on the Mountain" were among the many she continued to sing. As the sun set in the west and twilight time appeared, Dottie West, in her strong soprano voice, sang a solo rendition of "God be with You till we Meet Again". This was the finale! The full moon rose, illuminating Tiger Mountain which had been witness to the grandest "free" concert ever!

Sadly, this movie, "There's a Still on the Hill", was never released. Yet, those who participated in this singing session will always have wonderful memories of the personable and talented Dottie West in Tiger, Georgia.

# The Tiger Outhouse

*Background information: Before the development of inside plumbing and bathrooms, it was customary to have an outhouse. This was a small separate building, with a worn path, several yards away from the house, which had a bench with one or more round or oval holes and a pit beneath. This outside toilet was also called "the facility", a "privy", a "latrine", or a "sh--house". In some cases, the structure was suspended over a creek or stream, with "immediate flushing". In order to improve the health of the public, a project of the WPA (Works Project Administration) was to provide a more sanitary toilet with a concrete base, or slab, a "preformed throne" to cover the dug receptacle. Also, soft absorbent tissue paper was more available and used, instead of the thin sheets of the old catalog.*

In the spring of 1936, my grandfather Arrendale began a verbal campaign to have a new outhouse, a "two seater", built as the family size was fast increasing. Granddaddy had been slow to agree to this "dern female notion", but finally he relented. As the work crew arrived early one morning to begin spraying the apple orchard, Granddaddy's eyes lit up -- he had a PLAN! One of the hands was a differently-disabled young man, and he could manually dig the hole for the new toilet.

So, Grandma marked off the 6'x4' space, and she instructed the mentally challenged "hired helper" to dig until she told him to quit. Then, she told me that my younger cousin, Joanne, and I could watch, but I was not to let Joanne fall into the excavation; nor were we to hinder the "hired helper" in any way.

The digging process began. With each shovel full of red soil, the mound of dirt became bigger and higher. 8:00, 9:00, 10:00, 11:00 and soon the sun was high overhead for noon. The young man continued to shovel; the opening into the earth got deeper and deeper and deeper. As Joanne and I leaned over to peer into the depths of the empty space, we two expected to see a little Chinaman appear at any moment for we were positive that the "hired helper" was digging halfway to China!

Suddenly, from the kitchen, my grandma appeared! She dashed down the back porch steps, waving her apron and shouting. "Stop, Stop! Have mercy on us! STOP!" All she could see was the top of the black felt hat of the "hired helper", and the two "grands" who were covered with red Georgia clay!  It was now evident that the deepest toilet hole in the history of Tiger Mountain had been dug.

The immediate problem was how to get the "hired help" up and out; he could not climb out nor could he scale the sides of the hole. Grandma sent for a sturdy green kitchen chair which was placed onto the floor of the hole, and the "hired helper" slowly was able to get up and out -- no worse from the wear.  Soon thereafter, we three ate lunch and never did fried chicken and biscuits taste so good!

Within days, the wood construction of the two seater outhouse was completed, with a window, lattice-work, and iron latch on the door.  This new addition to the outbuildings on the farm was now finished.

In a few years, modernization had arrived with an indoor bathroom.  The "two-seater" was no longer of use and slowly rotted. Then, one day, a tractor pushed the old wooden structure into the "hired helper" hole -- gone but not forgotten.

My brother, Jim, now owns the old home place.  Each Spring the 6'x4' indention in the earth is apparent as violets, jonquils and tomato vines bloom around the site.  At family gatherings, we kinfolks often recall about the massive toilet hole that the "hired helper" dug on that sunny day long ago.

---

# Chapter 5
## Summer

# The Preacher's Wife and Lucifer

Years ago, a custom in these mountains was to invite the local pastor and his family for Sunday dinner after the morning worship service. There was a tentative schedule for who was responsible for feeding the preacher on any particular Sabbath. The minister assigned to the Tiger Church was a quiet man of small stature. His wife, Thelma Jo, was just the opposite; she was a large woman with a loud voice and a "painted up" face. The preacher's wife talked "without ceasing" and no one could get a word in edgewise!

In the early summer, it was a "turn" for Mrs. Lizzie Keason, the dedicated leader of the Tiger Methodist Church, to feed the preacher. (This was 1946, years before the addition of the "United" to the denomination's name.) On that Sunday, my mother, Clyde Ellen, sent me to help the widow Mrs. Keason finish preparing the meal. The dining room was seldom used except when the preacher came to dinner. The table was covered with a sparkling white linen cloth with matching napkins, and I placed the Sunday-best dishes and silverware for the four of us. While Mrs. Keason dished up the vegetables, fried chicken, gravy, and hot biscuits, I sliced fresh tomatoes and cucumbers. During this time, the Preacher's Wife, Thelma Jo, never, ever stopped talking! Mrs. Keason was becoming visibly irritated and mumbled to me, "Rattle, rattle, rattle."

Eventually, we were seated at the dinner table. The Preacher's Wife, Thelma Jo, did hush for the blessing, but immediately afterward, began a constant flow of chatter. After passing the food and serving our plates, we began to eat. Suddenly, there was a SILENCE -- a DEAD SILENCE. When we looked at Thelma Jo, she was ashen pale, her mouth open. She was gasping for breath and her eyes bulged with terror. With a trembling finger, the Preacher's Wife was pointing upward. High above, hanging from the ceiling rafter, was Mrs. Keason's four foot long pet blacksnake, Lucifer, watching every bite we took and every move we made. When Mrs. Keason saw her slender, harmless pet, she waved her hand and said, "Go to the barn, Lucifer. You heard me! Go now!" As instructed, Lucifer crawled down the wall, wiggled outside, and off to the barn he went.

The Preacher's Wife, Thelma Jo, was still in a state of shock, so fearful she could not eat. I helped the Preacher load up his panic-stricken mate, who was still unable to make an audible sound, into the car.

As the vehicle disappeared over the hill, Mrs. Keason, with a sly, knowing smile and twinkling eye declared, "Now we know that with Lucifer's help, the Preacher's Wife can be quiet and not speak a SINGLE word!"

---

Sunday dinner without Lucifer or Thelma Jo

# Girdling Down the Road

One of life's biggest problems for women, both young and old, is the proper procedures for the placement of the panty hose garment. However, this troublesome process is simple in comparison to the following experience of mine.

On a long ago summer day, we were traveling south to attend a musical performance by our talented grandson, Beau Taylor Bryan, at MGC auditorium, a five hour drive. Melvin was already dressed for the occasion, including having his necktie on and the false teeth in! I was all "gussied-up" in a new dress, but I decided to postpone the wearing of my new long-line panty girdle until we were at our destination.

Due to road construction and the slow traffic of a funeral procession, we were running late. I then decided to go ahead and put on my "body smoother" as we drove along. I successfully got both feet in the allotted spaces; however, in the cramped area of the front seat, it became most difficult to pull upward.

I began tugging, pulling, and twisting the hateful "body smoother", but to no avail! I was barely able to move as the new girdle had a strong grip on me.

Desperately, I located the lever to recline the car seat backwards, but this did not help matters at all! By now, my legs felt numb, and were a bluish color due to lack of circulation. My predicament worsened as the pull-on high waisted garment tightened on my midriff, waist, and back causing my breathing to become shallow.

Melvin started to pull over to the side of the interstate to assist me, but I wailed, "No! No! Don't Stop! Just keep on going. We can't be late for the recital." So I remained in the vise of my "body smoother" which had been advertised as non-binding, comfortable support -- (individual body measurements may vary).

Within the speed limit, we arrived on campus frantically searching for a parking space. Melvin dashed around to open the car door (first time since our courting days some forty years ago) and helped me up and out to the sidewalk. But another problem had developed! The hateful "body slimmer" had my knees bound together and I wobbled like a pigeon-toed duck. When daughter Dawne saw her mama struggling to walk, she immediately inquired, "What is wrong?"  To which I replied, "Just show me the ladies lounge.  My long-line girdle is warped!"

As the curtain arose, we were in our seats.  I was trim - and - slim, the "smoother" had done its work.  I was two sizes smaller and truly a great, big, beautiful doll.

..........................................................................................................

## Girdle II: Girdling in the Air

A telephone call was received from my cousin in eastern North Carolina that our beloved Aunt Pauline had passed away.  As soon as the funeral arrangements were complete, my brother, Jim Pleasants, offered to fly the three of us, Mama Clyde, him, and me, to the services in the Centerville community in Franklin County N.C.  Jim instructed us to meet him at the Toccoa Airport early on Friday morning.  He further stated that Mama and I would be more comfortable getting in and out of the airplane if we wore slacks.  So, we two chose to dress in black pantsuits.  Mama insisted that we carry along, for warmth, a quilt; the pattern was appropriately named "Trip Around the World".  Since I was to see numerous kinfolks, I felt it necessary to look my very best.  I decided to wear my new pants liner (or long girdle) that was a waist to ankle support garment of nylon, spandex, and elastic lace.

Mama Clyde and I arrived at the airport just minutes before the tan single engine Cherokee taxied back down the runway.  We boarded, and Mama settled into the passenger seat beside Jim.  I squeezed into the limited space of the back seat carrying the heirloom quilt.

As we gained altitude, my claustrophobia became most pronounced.  So, I covered myself head and all with the "security" quilt.  Unable to speak, I could hear the conversation from the cockpit as Mama, the co-pilot, studied the map and flight routes.  I recall her urging me to view the city of Charlotte, the Raleigh-Durham area, and to see the Boeing 727 whose flight path was very close.  I could not look!  Upon landing, relatives met us, and we motored to attend the church services and burial of Aunt Pauline.  Afterwards, we took off for the flight back to North Georgia. As the airplane cruised along at 110 miles per hour, I developed a medical crisis! Both of my legs began to have most painful muscle cramps. My suffering became so severe that my only hope was to remove the tight pants liner. Still in my quilt cocoon, I began by first removing my black dress pants. This was not too difficult. The chatter from the front seat continued, so I had not disturbed Jim or Mama. Next, I decided to begin the process of removing the hateful pants liner. I tugged at the left side, and as I pulled downward and my weight shifted, the plane rapidly banked to the right. Then, I attempted to remove the right leg. As I struggled, the plane sharply shifted to the left. The plane continued to rock and roll as I tried to shed the aggravating girdle garment.

Still covered by my quilt, I heard mumblings from the cockpit as to the unusual movement of the plane. Jim checked the instrument panel, a veteran Marine fighter pilot who has been licensed for thirty years, he was becoming very CONCERNED. After a stunned silence, I heard my brother call, "Janie P. are you OK?" To this I replied, "No, my leg muscles are cramping and I am taking off this pants liner by wiggling and wagging, back and forth!"

"Hallelujah!" Jim exclaimed. "I was afraid that some sort of mechanical failure had caused me to lose control and I was about to call 'Mayday, Mayday'!" Soon, the black dress pants were back on, and the discarded "slimmer" lay in a heap on the floor. From beneath my quilt, I heard Jim remark that the Blue Ridge Mountains were in view. Excitedly, I threw off my cover to see the scenery. Immediately, without any warning, I saw human bodies hurling downward. Petrified, I wondered if I was on my way to the heavenly gates as bodies fell to eternal burning. Back under my security quilt I went, seeing my life pass before me. From the radio Jim learned that sky divers from UGA and Clemson were free falling, practicing for the air show at the college football game the next day.

After a picture perfect landing, we made our way back to the beautiful mountain named Tiger, my haven, the source of my strength, and the place of much that I treasure.

---

# What's in a Name?

As our family awaits the arrival of a third great-grandchild, much time and energy has been expended in the selecting of a name. Names are special as they belong to that person and identify their very being! As a teacher, I learned early on to respect and correctly pronounce the name of each student. Much careful consideration and deliberation should be given to the choosing of a name for an infant.

My GIVEN NAME is Janie, which has a family connection. The late Jane Arrendale Bramlett was a talented mountain mother and wife who created woolen cloth and coverlets from her spinning wheel and weaving loom.

My MAIDEN NAME is Pleasants. My father, Miles Otis Pleasants, was a native of Franklin County in eastern North Carolina, and the name originated from the early settlers who migrated from England.

My SURNAME, now, is that of my husband, John Melvin Taylor, who was the NAMESAKE of his beloved uncle John Harley Taylor. (Yes, the Laurel reader is correct: I do not have a MIDDLE NAME.)

My sister, Margaret Pleasants Thrasher, has the NICKNAME of "Peggy", a traditional name inherited from two ancestral grandmothers. My only brother, James Virgil Pleasants, was the first male grandchild on my mother's side--complete with the Arrendale clear blue eyes! He was named after both grandfathers respectively, James Patrick Pleasants and John Virgil Arrendale. However, James was soon shortened to Jim!

The choosing of a name for the first male Arrendale cousin resulted in a family conference. Three generations gathered around the birthing-room bed of the mother, reviewed the genealogy of the Arrendale clan, and all agreed on the name William Bruce. This was in the year of 1946.

I have often wondered about the first name of my grandmother, Tallulah Ellen Edwards Arrendale. Family historians relate that her name "Tallulah" came about in this manner: John C. Edwards, her father, was a veteran of the War Between the States. Prior to this civil war, he had a family of seven children (the first set), and upon returning home he had six more (the second set). My grandmother was the 11th child of 13 siblings.

An older son, Duncan, became a circuit-riding preacher assigned by the Methodist Church to this Northeast Georgia region. In the spring of 1876, his father, John C. Edwards, made a trip by horseback to visit his minister son. While traveling the Methodist circuit from one church meeting to another, the father and son viewed the most beautiful land district above a river about two miles north of the waterfalls, lush and green with colorful mountain laurel and rhododendron, evergreens, and moss growing on the rocks.

Seeing this landscape, John C. Edwards asked the name of this spectacular tract. He was told "Tallulah," at which time he stated, "My next daughter to be born will be named Tallulah!" On January 17th, 1878, a girl-child was delivered and so named. The Cherokee Indian name is Tälutti; and there are differing translations and meanings but to our family "Tallulah" means beautiful, graceful, and lovely.

Sometimes, the source, or origin, of a name remains a mystery. For example, my mother was named CLYDE Ellen Arrendale to honor an aunt, CLYDE Abernathy Edwards. As a talented seamstress, Aunt Clyde had designed and hand-sewn the trousseau garments for her sister-in-law, Tallulah. On the day of the wedding, my grandmother asked of Aunt Clyde, "How can I ever repay you for making me these beautiful outfits?" To which Aunt Clyde replied, "Just promise me that your first daughter will be named for me!"

And so it was! Clyde is not an uncommon name for a male, but rather unusual for a woman. Being of Scots-Irish descent, perhaps the name came from those who had lived near the river of Clyde in Scotland -- but no one knows for sure!

Over the ridge and in the next hollow from our home lived the McClain family. The parents, Rosa May (Bleckley) and Ray McClain had been most creative in naming their eight children with rhyming middle names. In order of their birth are: Dorothy Fay (Duncan), Mildred May (Chlupacek), Hugh Jay, William Ray, Zane Gray, Dean Gay, David Kay, and Michael Clay.

Being a most unusual occurrence, Ripley's "Believe It or Not" listed this during the 1940's.

My fondest memories of the McClains is of the family sitting together on the long wooden pew in the old Baptist Church in Tiger, all cleaned up and smelling of "Sweetheart" soap, and all singing, with much gusto, the beloved hymn, "Heavenly Sunshine".

Editors Note: As the *Laurel* goes to press, we have been informed that the new baby boy has arrived and his name is Michael Parker Cox -- all family names!

# "Bean Man" Knew His Teeth

On a sunny warm afternoon, Melvin, also known as "The Bean Man of Rabun" was on his way home to Tiger. He decided to stop and visit with his friend, Bert, at the car dealership on Main Street. A shipment of new '72 Chevrolets had just arrived. Rolling off the car carrier was a shiny vehicle, the same green color as the leaves of a bean plant. Furthermore, the interior of his automobile was a soft green tone, like the young beans that hung on the vine.

Smitten, Melvin wrote a check and purchased the "green bean car" for his wife, Janie P.

Great was the excitement when Melvin arrived home with his new horseless carriage. Soon the time arrived for the two to get ready and "all gussied up" to attend the wedding of the local district attorney's daughter at 7:00 at a Clayton Church.

The couple looked real "spiffy" in the green bean car and were very mannerly and polite as they greeted friends and kin. After the ceremony, Janie P. and Melvin motored out to the reception being held at Kingwood, which had just been renovated and was back in business again. The decorations were lovely, the bride radiant, the groom glowing with pride, the food very tasty, and the fountain of champagne flowed freely.

Between flutes of the bubbly, Melvin took friends out to see his gift to Janie P., the green bean car.

As the band began to play "oldie but goodie" tunes, the couple enjoyed dancing. However during the rendition of the "Tennessee Waltz", the Bean Man began to feel the effects of too much of the "effervescent spring water", and became slower in movement until he gradually sank to the dance floor. Lying there, limp, Melvin looked up and, with a big smile, he said, "Best d___ champoo I ever drunk!"

Our friends, a local county commissioner and his wife, who were dancing nearby, edged over to assist Janie P. in the rescue operation; that was to remove the Bean Man off the floor and get him out the kitchen door. Outside, the three lugged him up a concrete flight of steps to the parking area and, finally, into the green bean car.

Having been in possession of her new car for only a few hours, Janie P. had not even been behind the steering wheel. In the darkness, the iginition key was found in the Bean Man's coat pocket. When Janie P. started the engine, the instrument panel lit up, but, at the same time, there were loud sounds ... buzzings... ding-donging... and bells ringing. Mercifully, by pushing buttons and pulling levers, the noises ceased. The driver released the emergency brake, adjusted the headlights, fastened the seat belts and the couple left the country club and were on their way home.

But wait!!

As they motored up the mountain towards town, Melvin woke up from his nap saying, "I'm sick. Quick!" By sheer luck, Janie P. located the correct button to push and the car window beside Melvin opened. Immediately, all of the "champoo" was deposited on the shoulder of Highway 76 East.

The next morning, after his first cup of coffee, Melvin asked, "Where are my teeth, Janie P." and he began searching for his "party teeth", but to no avail. Then the sick stop on the way home the previous night was recalled. With Melvin driving the green bean car, which still smelled new, they returned to the scene and began searching for the missing items.

All other evidence was gone, except there in the grass were the "pearly whites"! Picking up his teeth, Melvin brushed them off, wiped them on his pants, then popped them into his mouth and yelled, "They fit good. They must be mine!"

Melvin and Janie P. Taylor in 2008

# The President, the Secret Service and Janie P.!

With the passing of the 40th President of the United States, Ronald Wilson Reagan, I recall the one occasion in which I saw, in person, then President Reagan and his wife, Nancy. This occurred at the opening day ceremonies of the 1982 World Fair in Knoxville, Tennessee. This exposition was located at the site of an old mill village on hilly terrain. A fast moving creek flowed underneath an old stone bridge. New buildings had been constructed and pavilions spotlighted countries and nations of the world.

When I arrived early on that May morning, security forces were in place. (Since Mr. Reagan had been hit by an assassin's bullet a few months earlier, his protection was of great concern.) Having no camera nor gun, I was cleared to enter the grounds. Since I was determined to see our national leader, Mr. Reagan, I found a spot near the Panama exhibit with excellent visibility of the parade route. A standing group of us gathered in a metal-fence enclosed area to wait and watch for the presidential motorcade to slowly drive by on the road below. As the minutes passed, we folks discussed our hometowns and native states. We also observed the rapid acceleration of police protection as S.W.A.T. teams were most concerned about the safety of President Reagan -- particularly around the old bridge structure. A Secret Service Agent, with eyes as blue as steel, was constantly scanning this territory. Suddenly, two men who were chatting most excitedly in Spanish, dashed out of the pavilion and rushed into the lower level. Within seconds, we were surrounded by the S.W.A.T. team and the Secret Service Agent, with steel blue eyes, looked at me and demanded, "Do you speak Espanol?" To this, I answered, "No, I don't speak the language." Then I declared, "I'm from Tiger, Georgia." Then the crowd behind me echoed, "She's from Tiger. She is from Tiger, Georgia and she doesn't know Spanish!"

By this time, the group from Panama was able to clarify their activities by simply stating that the bathroom commode would not flush and repairs were needed.

In the distance, the motorcade was seen slowly moving toward our area. Then, a little boy in our group cut his hand on the metal fence. As the parents rushed him to the first aid station, they handed me (the grandmotherly type) the blue diaper bag to hold. I was immediately surrounded by the S.W.A.T. team and the National Guard.

As I tried to explain, the Secret Service agent with steel blue eyes dashed up. When he saw me, he lost his trained composure; his eyes twinkled and a slight smile appeared, and he said, "It's okay. She's from Tiger, Georgia." Again, the spectators behind me chanted, "Yes, she is from Tiger, Georgia."

The Presidential car, carrying President Reagan and the First Lady, now appeared and passed in front of us. As we cheered, we received a "thumbs up", a wave and a blown kiss from Nancy herself. As we watched the motorcade proceed, we saw the Secret Service agent with steel blue eyes trotting alongside the limousine.

Twenty-two years have passed. During the week of tribute to the late President Reagan, I'm sure I saw the same Secret Service agent protecting the widow. Much older and with graying hear, he was constantly surveying the mourning crowds. I assume he had been assigned to the Reagans and had been with them throughout the years and now will be very watchful over the former First Lady, Nancy Reagan.

# Pay-back Time

When we first cousins were youngsters here at Tiger Mountain, our uncle Joe Arrendale was a student at the Medical College of Georgia. Therefore, the seven of us were exposed to the latest information and current procedures in preventative health care, including flu shots, typhoid vaccinations, and "de-worming" liquid medications.

Before returning to Augusta on a Sunday afternoon in July, Uncle Joe announced that the time had arrived for the annual typhoid inoculations. Dressed in his white intern jacket, stethoscope around his neck and smelling strongly of rubbing alcohol, Dr. Joe instructed his nieces and nephews to line up for the SHOT!

Always at the front and first in line was Jim, who pushed up his shirt sleeve and stood still for the injection. He received accolades of praise for his bravery and being such a "big boy". Next, Joanne slowly stepped forward, prepared for the "pain and suffering" of the dreaded inoculation.

Then the eldest, Janie P. –– very apprehensive but determined, received the injection.

As the line decreased in number, John slowly inched his way backwards toward the end. Some of us noticed that he had placed both hands into the opposite sleeve of his long-sleeved shirt. When John tightly crossed his arms, the strait-jacket effect was achieved. He was protected so that no shot needle could be inserted.

Next, sweet and gentle Lucy stepped forward and took her "dose of medicine".

Peggy held the hand of Little Henry to comfort him, as both received the injection.

It was now John's turn! As he moved forward, he saw his chance to escape. John ran out the door, down the front steps, and raced away down the driveway, moving as fast as his skinny long legs could travel. Behind him was his ever faithful cousin, Jim, swiftly following, while hollering, "Run, John. Run!"

As these two dashed away, Uncle Joe, with the dreaded needle still in his hand, chased them. Then all of us cousins, two dogs, and the old yellow cat formed a single-file procession which passed by the creamery building and on down the farm road to the barn.

John immediately headed for the barn loft and plunged deep into the loose hay, hiding from the feared vaccination. The procession halted — only Jim knew where John was hidden. Uncle Joe, very visible in his white coat, waited for John.

Eventually John jumped out of the barn loft and circled the oak trees on top of the hill. Seeing a chance to outwit his elders, John swiftly rushed to the back door of his house, and with the speed of lightning, dived into the moth-ball filled woolen closet head-first. Nothing was visible but the behind of John.

As soon as Uncle Joe spotted him, he pulled down John's trousers and injected the dreaded vaccine, not into his nephew's left arm, but into his left buttock!

Mission completed.

We then enjoyed cold watermelon and John got the first slice as he was the only cousin to get a shot in the fanny.

Family stories such as this remain basically the same but they get better and better with each retelling, until these tales becomes legends as with "the day John ran from the needle".

I recall one special time when a member of the listening audience said to Aunt Rosebud, "Do you really believe this tale by Janie P.?" Smiling, she nodded her head and stated, "Oh, yes, I do. I was right there on the front porch."

Time passed by. Years later, I was "laid-up" at Mama's house with a most severe upper respiratory infection. Amidst my coughing and sneezing, I heard my Uncle Joe report that a double shot of antibiotics was needed. At about this time, John Ezzard, now a senior at med school, walked in the front door. Uncle Joe halted, his blue eyes twinkled and a large grin appeared on his face as he hollered, "Come on, John, now it's payback time for Janie P. Serves her right for telling the tale about you and the typhoid shot over the years."

Recalling past experiences and fearing the worst, I pulled the bed covers tightly around my neck. I anxiously awaited and anticipated that the shot would be administered in the largest muscle of my thigh, but, no, John painlessly popped the needle into my left arm. To this day, that was the most painless injection I have ever received.

"Pay-back time" had come and gone!

This story is dedicated to the many readers who, too, have a dreaded fear of being jabbed.

# Truck-driving Angels

The weather on that summer afternoon was hot and humid with thunderheads gathering in the sky. As I drove out of the driveway from the home of my daughter in middle Georgia, I heard a distant rumble. Soon, I saw streaks of lightning, and the first raindrops began to fall. By the time I reached the four-lane highway, the storm was raging. Hailstones were hitting the car, sharp lightning lit up the sky, and deafening rolls of thunder shook the earth. Slowly inching along, I saw an opening into the north flow of traffic, and I found myself behind a red International tractor-trailer. When I glanced into the rear-view mirror, I saw a loaded Mack logging truck. Following this was a long procession of car lights--truly a slow-moving parking lot. Conditions worsened, and then I realized that the two truck drivers were looking out for me and my safety. The one in front would signal that deep-ponded water was ahead, or that large amounts of rainfall was rushing across the highway, forcing us to slow down to zero miles per hour. Occasionally, we could speed up, but mainly we just "moseyed along" mile after mile.

Vivid memories of another time and place came to me. When I was nine years old, my Mama Clyde and I were caught in a similarly terrifying situation. Why were we two out traveling in such weather? Mama and I had journeyed to Athens to bring back a car load of apples, which had been in cold storage for home use and local sales. My grandfather, John V. Arrendale, was an orchardist here at Tiger Mountain. During the peak of the apple season, five hundred or more bushels would be hauled to cold storage units in Athens to be marketed during the winter months. The black four-door 1934 Ford was soon loaded, and we were on the way back to the mountains.

As we drove up the road, the sky darkened. Then, there was a stillness, and the eerie electrical green light warned us that this was "the calm before the storm". Gusts of wind shook the car, thunder boomed overhead, streaks of lightning surrounded us, and pellets of hail bounced off the windshield. A cloudburst, or sudden flood of rain, had occurred. Then, my Mama Clyde began singing the beloved hymn of care and assurance, "God Will Take Care of You".

I joined in and, a bit off-key, we sang the verses and refrain over and over again.

Be not dismayed whate'er betide, God will take care of you;
Beneath His wings of love abide, God will take care of you.
God will take care of you, Through every day, O'er all the way;
He will take care of you, God will take care of you.

I was 40 years of age when I realized that my Mama Clyde was not singing to comfort me, but for strength herself as she was so frightened and concerned for our safety on the lonely stretches of road in Banks County. To this day, I am positive that there was a Guardian Angel sitting on each of the four fenders, and that another was hovering over the hood of the car, which kept us free from harm. Gradually, the storm diminished, and as we approached the town of Cornelia, the sun broke through the clouds and a most brilliant rainbow was visible.

Back to reality, I began to hum and sing the hymn of trust and guidance as we traveled along--the semi, me, and the log truck. Approaching the I-20 junction, the driver of the 18-wheeler blinked his lights, honked the horn and waved goodbye. The logging truck and I kept on moving. Then I heard a horn, saw the turn signals, and the driver gave a "thumbs-up" farewell as he exited to a woodyard off of I-85.

I will never know the name, race, creed or religion of the two Guardian Angels who protected me. I do know that I am grateful to these two men and to all professional truck drivers who have given a helping hand, or provided emergency assistance, or pulled the air-horn at children along the way. I salute the operators of all "big rigs".

# Janie P. and the Fishing Trip

When Melvin and I married in 1962, I felt that "togetherness" was of great importance. So, at the first hint of "going fishing," I was positive this was a chance to strengthen our marriage by being together. To me, "going fishing" meant a picnic, a swim, a tanning session, fishing for fun--just enjoying the outing. But, NO, this was not my new mate's concept at all! "Going fishing" to Melvin meant launching a boat into the lake, drifting along for hours without making a sound nor any movement to disturb the fish below. Complete silence was essential. Also, it was necessary to wear dark clothing to prevent shadows on the water.

Over the years, Melvin has been known as "Bream" Taylor because he has caught so many bream and fish of all types from the streams and lakes of Rabun County. Reports have been heard that if Melvin is behind in the number of fish caught, he will maneuver the boat and his fishing buddy into the bushes where buddy will be unable to cast out or hang a fish! To put it mildly, serious fishing was of prime importance. Even as Burton Lake was filling up, Melvin, a little fellow, would go fishing with his dad, from the bank, on the condition that he would tote the fish home. The father-son duo would catch so many, that on the walk home, the tails of the fish would be dragged off.

On the Saturday we were to be quietly married, Melvin and his best man went fishing near Burton Bridge. Suddenly the two realized that they were hours late leaving the lake. Sitting on the porch steps in my wedding outfit, I waited and waited. Tearfully I assumed that I'd been "stood up at the altar". Then Melvin arrived with a corsage and lengthy excuses and great apology. However, we made the trip to meet the judge at the courthouse in Walhalla, South Carolina just before closing time.

Our first fishing trip together began early on that July morning. The boat was launched with the 10 hp Johnson motor in perfect condition. The rods and reels, bait buckets, lunch, and all the needed items were on board. Immediately, I cast out with a spring lizard for bait and hung a three-pound largemouth bass. My new husband was very pleased with my fishing ability, and he placed the bass on a stringer tied to the oar lock. As we drifted along, I caught another bass about the same size as the first. As the fish cut water and jumped ferociously to expel the hook, Melvin netted him, and onto the stringer the second fish was placed. The two glared up at us as we motored along, and there was some mumbling being heard about "beginner's luck."

As the sun rose higher in the sky, I hooked another fine bass. The scowls and frowns were evident, as Melvin had not even had a bite. Now there were three bass on the stringer taunting Melvin as they floated beside the boat. Being frustrated by not catching anything, Melvin decided that I should captain the boat, running the motor, and paddling. As I steered the boat towards the bank, Melvin began hollering, "You have put me into these branches of this beech tree and I can't even throw out!" My response was to cast out, but unfortunately, the fish hook caught on Melvin's hat. Now his favorite John Deere cap was floating down the lake. During this commotion, I grabbed the outboard motor throttle. Not being too familiar with boating, I caused the motor to run aground on a nearby sand bar. It was spinning, grinding, and sputtering sand. There was no more silence now; just loud yelling, hollering, and swearing. My main concern was for the loss of lunch which was sinking below the surface. All the time, three bass on the stringer gently floated along sneering upward.

Since the bait bucket was upside down, the dinner lost, and "Bream" Taylor's pride damaged, Melvin said it was time to leave as the ski boats would be coming out and the lake would become rough and fishing poorer. (In other words, this "togetherness" was not for him.) We loaded the boat and the stringer with three bass still glaring at us.

On the long drive back, Melvin declared to me, "If I manage to survive to get home to Tiger, I will never, ever take you fishing with me again!" And he didn't for the next 35 years until one morning -- but that is another story.

---

# The Charleston June Wedding

Since the month of June is traditionally a time of weddings, I recall that in 1969, we received a most formal invitation to attend the wedding of an Arrendale cousin, Bruce, to the lovely Alicia. The bride, of Charleston, South Carolina, was a member of an old and aristocratic family.

The Daughters Three, Mama Clyde, and I traveled from Tiger Mountain to the coast to mix and mingle with kinfolks and the low country elite.

That evening, we gathered for the rehearsal dinner. A very elaborate meal was served with a special Irish drink called mead, a fermented honey-applejuice beer. Immediately, the Elder Ones forbade the Daughters Three and me to even taste this concoction! Remember that the older generation had been reared in the strict Methodist vow of total abstinence, and that all alcoholic beverages were sinful. "Teetotalers" they were!

On the next day, we attended the wedding ceremony at the historic church on the cobblestone street near the waterfront of Charleston. The colors, radiating from the large stained glass windows were repeated in the outfits of the weddings attendants -- truly magnificent!

The Daughters Three and the Arrendale relatives were most presentable and the behavior was outstanding. The Elder Ones were pleased.

The wedding reception was held in the ballroom of the luxurious hotel downtown. A bountiful buffet was being served and in the center of this area was an ornate flowing fountain, a giant gushing waterfall of champagne. However, placed in one corner was a cut-glass bowl of nonintoxicating fruit juices now referred to as the "Arrendale punch".

Daughters Three decided to forgo the punch. Instead, each began sampling the bubbly liquid from the fountain which appeared to be clear mountain spring water. Neither The Elder Ones, nor I, noticed that much was being consumed by the Daughters Three who were unaware of its effects.

Later, the music and dancing began. Cousin Bill rushed to me and excitedly whispered that a problem was developing! On the other side of the ballroom, we located Oldest Daughter in the midst of the "highfalutin" guests. She was sitting on the knee of a senator admiring his moustache and lamb chop sideburns. We managed to get her towards the door, away from the bubbly drink and the eyes of the Elder Ones. Then, the behavior of the Youngest Daughter became of great concern. Waving champagne flute, taking high steps (like a Tennessee Walker) and loudly announcing that she was going to dive into the hotel pool and take a swim.

Seeing the situation, my brother, Jim, came to help with the rescue efforts and to shield the Daughters Three from the wrath of the Elder Ones. We then realized that one Daughter was missing! In the downstairs lobby, standing on an antique mahogany coffee table, was the Middle Daughter loudly proclaiming, "Take me home to Black Rock Mountain State Park!" We managed to get the Daughters Three to the garage area and into a car for the ride to Jim's house and away from the disapproving eyes of the Elder Ones. Due to the excitement and large number of guests, their absence was never noticed!

During the long ride home on the next day, I would hear an occasional moan and groan from the backseat. The Daughters Three were suffering a most severe hangover with dizziness, headaches, and nausea. As the miles clicked away, Mama Clyde commented, "The girls are certainly quiet this morning. They must be worn-out from the wedding doings." I simply replied, "Yes, indeed!"

The Elder Ones are no longer with us, the fruit punch has never been replaced by wine from the grape vineyard. The Daughters Three learned a very valuable lesson concerning the over-consumption of alcoholic spirits. Today, some 36 years later, the Daughters Three remain sober, church going, God fearing and yes, "teetotalers" -- and the Elder Ones would approve!

Oh, and the newly married couple lived happily ever after.

Dawne Bryan, Daughter 2; Becky Ray, Daughter 3; Judy Scott, Daughter 1

91

# LeRoy, the Lucky Black Cat

Every family has treasured yarns and tales about a beloved pet. This account is about LeRoy, a cat who was the constant companion of my son, Wesley, for many years. Even the birth of LeRoy was no ordinary happening! As Wesley's wife, Karen, rested on the couch, wrapped in a cozy, soft blanket, she realized the mama cat, Charlotte, had climbed behind her. Suddenly Karen was aware of a warm, moist feeling at her back and she heard a tiny meow sound. A male kitten had been born, the first of Charlotte's litter. LeRoy had come to stay!

From that day on, LeRoy was special. He was a gentle, lively, healthy kitten who grew into a beautiful adult cat with shiny black fur with a few splotches of white. LeRoy was friendly, highly intelligent, and very independent. LeRoy loved to ride, sitting beside Wesley, as they traveled in the truck.

One summer day, Wesley called to ask if Melvin and I could "cat-sit" for LeRoy for several weeks as he and Karen were scheduled to be out-of-town. When we readily agreed, my instructions were: (a) that LeRoy was to never, ever have table scraps nor any food other than his own brand of cat food, (b) that LeRoy was to come and go, inside or out, as he wished, and (c) that LeRoy was to be allowed to rest and sleep whenever and wherever he so desired.

So LeRoy came to Tiger Mountain for his "vacation". He immediately adjusted to his new surroundings and became a great hunter and stalker. All was well for the first week until the late hours on Friday. Upon hearing loud squalling sounds with bumps and knocks, I jumped out of bed to see LeRoy in a state of convulsion, wreathing, crying mournfully, and tumbling down the hall. He then collapsed behind Melvin's recliner. Presuming LeRoy to be dead, I began sobbing, "I followed my three instructions! How can we tell Wesley?" Melvin simply said, "Go back to bed, and I'll bury LeRoy in the morning." Then, with an anguished howl and spasmodic movements, he awakened and struggled to the door. Of course, I had to let him go outside (because I had promised) and into the swamp LeRoy fled.

For two days, we searched for the missing cat. We so dreaded telling Wesley that LeRoy had disappeared. Late on Sunday, I heard a feeble "meow" at the front door, and I saw an exhausted and weak

LeRoy. He staggered as he tried to walk, his head tilted to one side, and his eyes did not focus. When Melvin saw this pitiful creature, he said, "I don't care what Wesley says, feed this poor cat all the sardines he can eat."

When Wesley next called, I told him that LeRoy was "not well". To this, Wesley replied that, by first light, they would come for his pet and take LeRoy to visit his own veterinarian in Habersham.

After an exam, and a discussion concerning LeRoy's stay in the mountains at the home place with rocky creeks flowing on three sides, the Vet diagnosed the problem: LeRoy had been poisoned by eating an excessive number of "blue-tailed lizards" (also known as a skink, newt, or salamander) which are native to this area. Cats crave this delightful delicacy for these amphibians produce a psychedelic effect on the nervous system, like an LSD high. The vet was totally amazed that his patient, LeRoy, had survived for in the words of Melvin, "He musta shurley have 'et a bait of 'em!"

In one day or so, the recovering LeRoy returned to complete his stay with us. As soon as he arrived, he began sniffing and smelling for -- you guessed it! -- another delicious poisonous "blue-tailed" lizard. But, to no avail, LeRoy has annihilated and destroyed the population of little creatures!

As fall arrived, LeRoy returned to his home, not the worse from wear.

---

LeRoy

## "Excuse me!  Excuse me!  Please pardon us!"

Over the years my daughter Becky and her family have made a yearly trek to Myrtle Beach, South Carolina, for a week of rest and recreation. The summer of 1981, however, is the most memorable. Vince and Brooks, the twins, were four years old, and Whitney was a babe in arms.

The travel weather on Sunday was stormy, and the cold rains continued on Monday, Tuesday, Wednesday, Thursday, and Friday. There had been no "fun in the sun", no swimming or picnics, and certainly no golf games for Mike.

After the time of togetherness spent in the motel room with three active youngsters, Becky had a plan. She insisted that her husband, Mike, go tour the local golf pro shops and she would take the children to see the movie "Annie" that Saturday.

After purchasing one adult ticket, Becky and her three entered the lobby. Since there was a special price on a small bucket of hot buttered popcorn along with a super-size iced cola, she bought these for each of the boys.

By this time, the matinee had already started. They entered the darkened theater, which had a large center section, two aisles, and the usual sloping floor, and it was almost filled to capacity on this rainy day. Finally, three vacant seats were spotted down and in the very middle of the section. Slowly, from the right aisle, Becky, who was carrying Whitney, the diaper bag, and her pocketbook was followed by the twins, who were lugging their colas and popcorn. They made their way to their seats saying, "Excuse us. Excuse us. Pardon us!" To the great relief of the other patrons, they finally settled down to watch the movie.

Shortly thereafter, a distinctive odor prevailed, and it became evident that Whitney needed a diaper change. Becky whispered to the twins for them to remain seated, to be quiet, and that she would return soon. Becky proceeded to go out the left aisle, carrying Whitney, the diaper bag, and her pocketbook, constantly repeating, "Excuse me. Excuse me. Please pardon us." The movie watchers are groaning, moaning, and sighing with resignation at this interruption.

When Becky and Whitney left the changing room, there were the two boys, still dragging the colas and popcorn. Wide-eyed with distress, Vince announced that a strange man had spoken to him, and he had to tell his mother. (I've often wondered what the strange man said. It was probably, "Sit still and hush.")

Once again, Becky with Whitney, the diaper bag, the pocketbook, and the two boys, with the remains of popcorn and colas, returned to their seats from the right aisle saying, "Excuse me. Excuse me. Please, please pardon us!"

All was well until Brooks whispered, "Momma, your pocketbook dropped upside down and everything has fallen out!" With that, the two boys slid down out of their seats and began crawling along the floor for the contents of the spilled purse, which were rolling downward toward the front of the theater. As the twins tried to locate the keys, lipstick, billfold, and other items, they were scrambling under and around the seats among sticky candy wrappers, stale popcorn, and even a few mice droppings! When they brushed against the legs and shoes of the other movie patrons, both politely said, "Excuse me. Excuse me. Pardon us!" (By this time, the audience is no longer watching the movie, but observing, with great interest, this sideshow, which was free of charge.)

Becky is now squeezed down between the seats begging the boys to return and whispering that when the movie is over and the lights come on, the contents of the pocketbook would be found.

Sure enough, when the movie was over, the theater manager and his staff helped collect the remaining objects from the pocketbook. Becky, carrying Whitney, the diaper bag, and her purse, along with the very tired twins, made their way outside where Mike was waiting. Much to his astonishment, Becky began wailing, "Why did you leave me alone with these three children?" Then laughing, she said, "As Big Melvin would say, 'You deserted me in the face of the enemy!!!'"

The twins are 26 years old and Whitney is 23. The family still journeys to Myrtle Beach for vacations; however, Becky refuses to go anywhere near the cinema for fear that someone might recognize her and recall the eventful time of, "Excuse me. Excuse me. Please pardon us!"

---

# The Alligator, Toddler, and Janie P.

On a warm, sunny, summer day my dog Toddler and I were at Grandma's house over at the base of Tiger Mountain. Toddler was a small black and white wire terrier that was my constant companion and best buddy. As usual, Grandma sent Toddler and me to get the daily mail from the mailbox over on the Syrup City Road, just outside of Tiger. We left the cabin, walked down the hill, playing in the sand, watching the flying birds, and checking on the anthills. Then we stopped by the willow tree in the swamp and began throwing pebbles into the water and watching it ripple. Then up the hill and over the gap we went to the mailbox. As instructed, I counted the pieces of mail, one newspaper and two letters, before sticking them into my back pocket.

Back over the gap we went, and Toddler and I trotted down the hill. When we came to the willow tree in the swamp, Toddler began barking frantically shoving against my feet. I looked to see if a mud turtle or a water moccasin was visible, but I saw neither. Then I saw IT! A large alligator was lying under the branches of the willow tree. As he opened and closed his massive jaws, I could see the rows of teeth and his beady black eyes. Toddler had known that danger lurked and had protected me from this ferocious creature. Needless to say, we ran the long route by the pasture and barn to the safety of Grandma's house.

As I went into the kitchen, I saw Grandma at the stove frying chicken as she prepared the noon meal for the work hands. I gave the mail to her, one paper and two letters. Then I said, "Grandma, there is an alligator under the willow tree in the swamp!" Before Grandma could answer, my Aunt Ruth exclaimed, "She doesn't know an alligator from an earthworm, and Janie P. needs her mouth washed out with soap, lye soap at that, for telling untruths."

Since Grandma was too busy for such, she told me to go sit in a rocking chair on the front porch and think about my sinful ways! So with Toddler by my side, I rocked. Now, Toddler and I knew that we had found an alligator, but who was going to believe us? Certainly not my Aunt Ruth! Then I remembered that the work hands, riding in a mule-drawn wagon, would come to the house for dinner. I knew that they would cross over the gap and drive down the hill. When the mules sensed the presence of that alligator under the willow tree in the swamp, well, somebody would believe me then.

Toddler and I waited and watched. Soon, we heard the creaking and rattling of the farm wagon as it crossed over the gap and came down the hill. Sure enough, when the mules saw the large reptile, they became frightened and out of control. My Uncle Joe jumped off the wagon, saw the alligator, and realized what caused the frantic behavior of the mules.

Uncle Joe ran to the cabin shouting. "The alligator has escaped from the Tiger Zoo and it's under the willow tree in the swamp!" With these words, my Grandma hugged me and started crying. "Janie P., you could have been eaten alive!"

The men folk went to the Tiger Zoo and notified the veterinarian. He immediately brought a '34 Ford pickup truck to load the alligator. The reason the alligator had not attacked Toddler and me was because he was suffering from a near heatstroke after wandering away from the zoo. The snout of the alligator was tied and, with the tail thrashing, it was loaded and returned to his pool, shade trees, and proper diet at the Tiger Zoo.

Later that day as we all were on the front porch of the house, my Aunt Ruth said to me, "I'm so thankful you were not injured and Toddler is indeed a hero!. I know that you know the difference between an earthworm and an alligator, but promise me Janie P. that you will never, ever tell a falsehood!" So, I promised, but I still tell my tales of Tiger. Today, some seventy years later, the green willow tree and the swamp still exist. The alligator and the zoo at Tiger have vanished with only vivid memories left for a few of us who can recall that eventful day at the Zoo of Tiger.

---

# Chapter 6
## Fall

# The Skirt, Sheets, and Calico

*Editor's Note: One of the things our readers like best about Janie P. Taylor's monthly column are her homespun memories of family life and growing up in a close-knit family. Three of her recollections are presented below, along with a note we received from one of her family members.*

In the mailbox, an invitation to an evening wedding was received, and I immediately responded "yes" to the RSVP. Since this was the most "high-falutin' event of the season," it was of great importance for me to look good. Thus, the search began for a suitable outfit.

Daughters Three had given me a lined crocheted top with satin trim in the color of chocolate, because they said "The color brown is the new black." Then I recalled that in the back of my closet there hung a vintage garment (as old as the hills); an ankle-length full skirt with a floral pattern in brown, sandshell, and tan tones, with an elastic waistband. This also matched my new brown suede shoes, and with a matching handbag of leather, my ensemble was complete. I was indeed stylishly dressed!

As I entered the church, I just "floated on in" as I was confident that my matching coordinated outfit was perfect for this happy occasion. Upon sitting down after the Processional, I sensed a "bing" as the elastic in the waistband disintegrated due to age. It was not London Bridge that was falling down, but it was my skirt, for sure!

Pondering on this turn of events, I decided to tuck the bulky skirt into the elastic waistband of my half-slip. After the Recessional, I smiled sweetly and greeted everyone so that the "inflated tire" around my middle would not be noticed.

At the reception, the half-slip gave way, and my skirt began slowly drifting downward towards the floor. Locating the kitchen door as a means of escape, I held on to the back of the hateful skirt with one arm and hand, while tightly clutching the front with the other arm and hand. The only way to carry my mini-bag was to just hold it between my teeth! Moving slowly behind columns and in shadows, I escaped the prying eyes of other guests.

Safely outside and under the cover of darkness, the skirt fell to the ground around my feet. I quickly grabbed up this mass of material, and threw it into a nearby waste container never to be seen again! I drove home modestly covered by the long half-slip.

To this day, I've never mentioned viewing the video nor looking at the photo album of this event for fear of the inevitable scenes of me and the vintage skirt!

* * * * *

On these early fall mornings, the bright sun rays hit the dew-covered grass, and millions of brilliant like diamonds shine. Soon the dew evaporates, the mist rises, and the sky appears blue and crystal clear. By noon, however, puffy clouds begin forming over the mountain. Soon these develop into thunderheads, and a rain shower occurs. At this time, I recall these happenings of days gone by.

Prior to the development of an automatic clothes dryer, each and every household had a clothesline. Solar energy and wind power were utilized to dry the freshly washed garments and linens hanging on the line. Regularly, Aunt Ruth did the family laundry very early and the clothesline was soon filled with the "wash" -- a shirt, an apron, or big white bedsheets - all held in place by clothespins.

We children, who played up at the Oak Trees, would hear Aunt Ruth call "Bring in the sheets! Bring in the sheets now! The raindrops are beginning to fall!"

On Sunday, at church services, we often sang the favorite hymn, "Bringing In The Sheaves". My brother, Jim, and my cousin, John, (at age 5) sat on the front bench at the old church house and sang as loud as they could, "Bringing in the sheets! Bringing in the sheets!" (The word SHEAVES had no meaning to the youngsters, but BRINGING IN THE SHEETS was of great importance.)

* * * * *

On a wet morning, a tiny kitten was found near the home of my sister, Peggy. The stray had calico-colored fur, was very bright-eyed, and seemed to be "smart". Before taking the kitty to the local animal shelter, Peggy checked with family members for a possible home. My three grandchildren "took to it" as did we adults, and Calico Cat became a multi-generational pet but only if the local vet checked out the kitty.

Upon learning that Calico did not have feline leukemia, Peggy decided that the kitten should have a complete health exam, with preventative shots so the three month old was here to stay! The vet bill totaled $117.00, so the cat is often called Calico 117.

Now a "teen-ager" cat, Calico 117 is a very loving, caring pet, who sleeps on the porch, jumping, climbing, running, and chasing leaves in the sunlight as she investigates her world!

Recently, while Renn, age 9, was quietly working on his go-cart, Calico 117 was playing nearby in the side yard at MaClyde's house. Suddenly, Renn saw a fast-moving shadow, heard a swooping sound as a red-tailed hawk dove (at up to 120 mph) from his perch on Tiger Mountain to pounce on Calico 117. As the "chickenhawk" seized the cat, Renn began running toward them yelling for his dad to help. Hearing voices and commotion, the hawk dropped his prey, who had survived the attack with only a claw scratch on one ear. Holding Calico 117 close, Renn quoted the old adage that a cat has nine lives, and stated, "In that case, Calico Cat has only eight lives left to go!"

\* \* \* \* \*

Now a Word From the Other Side

I have a tale to tell about the Storyteller: my big sister, Janie P. Taylor:

My birthday has just passed, and two days before the big day, I started getting cards and telephone calls, many from people I haven't seen for years. Family and friends, in-laws and outlaws -- I heard from so many.

The most-welcome deluge continued until well past the date. The great outpouring of goodwill was most gratifying and appreciated.

This whole scheme was Janie P.'s. She has embarrassed the family so many times telling her tales "out of school". In my eyes, she has redeemed herself, and I promise to encourage other members of the family to again recognize her as one of us.

I do sincerely thank each well-wisher for the greeting, and I thank my big sister for arranging this. We have a real treasure in "The Storyteller".

Jim Pleasants

# This Purple Made a Royal Mess

In 1957 the Russians launched the first spacecraft called "Sputnik", and the United States fell behind in space research and exploration! In order to "catch-up", the educational system began placing much emphasis on science. For several years afterward, federal funds were allocated to improve and strengthen the curriculum, and to provide more teaching aids and equipment for teachers at the local level.

Eventually the ordered items to improve science instruction began to arrive! As a teacher of science at the eighth grade level, my choice among the available new materials included a set of 36 supplementary textbooks (and the Teacher's Edition) titled *Everyday Problems in Science*.

My classroom was Room 5 in the old brick building of Rabun County High School in Clayton, (later demolished after a fire) and the room was furnished with six lab tables with six chairs at each table. There were large windows without screens, as the chairman of the Board of Education decreed that installing window screens was not a good expenditure of taxpayer money!

The textbook order arrived, was unpacked, and six copies were placed on each of the six lab tables. The delivery was made on a typical warm September day, indicative of the changing season. The red sumac and the yellow goldenrod were colorful, and the clumps of purple pokeberries were plump and juicy.

As class began, each eighth grader was instructed to examine the shiny new textbooks that were a supplementary resource to be used only during science period. They were not to be removed from the lab tables. The teacher discussed the proper care and usage of the hard-back edition. Next, the students and I reviewed the title page, the table of contents, and the glossary at the back of the book.

The assignment was then made for each student to read silently the "Introduction". Everyone was "on task" and the fall breeze blew through the wide-open windows. To my dismay, a bird flew into the classroom; no one saw the blue jay fluttering around the ceiling – very agitated at being captive in Room 5. I was holding my breath and being very concerned when suddenly the silence was broken by the voice of the most studious and polite boy in the class.

"Mrs. Taylor!!" Startled, the class looked up as the boy announced, "That d--- bird just (rhymes with fit) on this new science book!"

Spontaneous laughter erupted; the students and I collapsed at the sight of the purple colored mess which covered the entire page. The principal immediately entered the classroom fearing the worst, saw the vile glob on the new book, shook his head, smiled, and went on his way!

As the class resumed reading, I simply walked to the table with the ruined book and replaced it with the Teacher's Edition so the young man could continue reading.

Today, I'm positive that in the Great Used Textbook Depository in the sky, there is one new science book that is still dripping with pokeberry juice and "purple poop".

Rabun County High School, where Janie P. taught for many years

# Movie Star

When I retired from the "school teaching" game in 1987, I felt the need of a new avocation. An interesting, challenging, perhaps even profitable second career would, as the old folks say, "keep me out of the pool hall", and I would not have "idle hands", a most undesirable trait.

Immediately the opportunity of a lifetime presented itself! I had often thought of being a Hollywood actress (Hollywood, California, not the small hamlet of Hollywood on Hwy. 441). Now the movie *Foxfire* was to be filmed here in these mountains. Maybe my dream of making the Hollywood scene was about to become reality.

The director, Jud Taylor, and the movie crew soon arrived from California, and the search for cast members for the movie began. Up in Highlands I went for an audition and try-out. Much to my dismay, acting professionals from Atlanta got the speaking parts. However, a letter arrived telling me I had been selected as an extra for the western dance bar scenes. I was instructed to bring costumes -- cowgirl, square dance, and sundress outfits -- and to report on the following Tuesday for the filming of a *Foxfire* episode.

So, along with cast members John Denver, Jessica Tandy, and Hume Cronyn, we extras gathered at a local nightspot. The film director gave orders for the men to assemble on the right with the women on the left. They began selecting bar girls (with tiny, tiny waistlines), and customers (with average waistlines). Finally, everyone had been chosen except a large, tall male and me (who had no waistline at all). The director waved to us saying, "You two will be dance partners. Leave the floor taking eight steps and glide over and be seated at your table."

We began to practice over and over. Not just gliding, we "gludded" most expertly! At last the director yelled "Roll camera!" My partner and I gracefully left the dance floor, gliding the eight steps and were seated. On his mobile camera chair, the director maneuvered over to my partner and me, exclaiming with a broad smile, "You two were perfect, just wonderful."

I could sense the pending arrival of my movie contract at any moment! Then the director stated, "Both of you are of such large size, you blocked out the reflections of the mirror behind you, so these scenes took beautifully -- no blotches nor shadows on the film. Thanks for doing such a fine job blocking out the light."

Needless to say, I was very upset that I was not going to Hollywood for a movie career. To make matters worse, in the *Foxfire* movie, one can barely catch a glimpse of my partner and me gliding gracefully across the dance floor.

# Listen, my children, and you shall hear
## -- of our journey to the Boston pier.

Now that the days of September have arrived and vacation time is over, a most eventful trip is recalled. As a student of American history and with eligibility to be a member of the Daughters of the American Revolution, I was most interested in sightseeing in the Boston area. I wanted to trace the route of the famous ride of Paul Revere, drive along the Freedom Trail, visit the Old North Church, observe the harbor where our forefathers dumped the boxes of tea into the ocean as a rebellion against the unfair British taxations, and to view the swan and swan boats at the Boston Public Gardens.

Our journey north began. My family and I immediately became aware of a language barrier between the vernacular, or regional speech, of my Southern Appalachian heritage and the Yankee brogue. I could not understand such questions as, "Did I care for sugar or sweetener in my coffee?" I could only reply with an "eh" or an "uh" or "Pardon me". So, conversing with the native countrymen was "nigh unto impossible".

Our first objective was to visit the Commons area, which is located in the heart of downtown Boston. We were there during Independence Day and wanted to be a part of living history. The road map indicated an exit off of I-95. Simple enough, but we were not prepared for the massive highway interchange with three differing levels of I-95! In the heavy flow of traffic, we just took the first exit available, which steered us into the inner city. Up and down the hills and over former marshland we traveled--at about the same speed as Paul Revere!

Hours later, we saw huge DETOUR signs, as the connector tunnel known as the "Big Dig" was being constructed. A detour mattered not to us; we were lost anyway.

Eventually, we began to "honk and holler" for directions. The communication gap was too great. We were ignored until a kind soul "pointed" us to the Commons area.

As we motored toward downtown Boston, we found ourselves in the midst of a massive demonstration for a "Planned Parenthood, Anti-Abortion" rally. Hundreds of activists were waving banners, singing loudly, and marching down the streets. Stranded, we just watched the goings-on.

Finally, we arrived at the Boston Commons area. Immediately, Wesley spotted one of Boston's Finest: a large policeman, in full uniform, riding on a thoroughbred quarterhorse of bay color. Now is the time to ask for directions to travel north on I-95, decided Wesley. As he approached the lawman, Wesley commented on the magnificent saddle horse and then politely asked for assistance. To this the officer asked, "Where's y'cah?" Wesley, still pondering the majestic red-brownish horse with the black mane and tail, hastily replied, "Sir, my cows are down on my farm in Georgia, a herd of Black Angus."

To this, the formidable policeman on an equally-formidable horse glared down at my son. Raising his voice in demand, he said, "I said, where's y'cah? Where's y'vehicle?" Wesley, a bit confused and embarrassed, apologized. "Sorry sir, for my misunderstanding. The car is parked right over there." Without a smile, the cop gave us instructions. "Go up one block, turn left, and you will enter the north expressway." With this, the Boston policeman abruptly turned. He and his mount trotted away, never looking back.

Paul Revere traveled to Medford town and on to Lexington and over to Concord. We didn't. We could not find the way. We missed many of the sites we had hoped to visit.

Soon, we did make the trip back to Tiger Mountain. Here, our "kin and friend" could tell the difference between "cow" and "car".

# I Really Educated That Guy

The year was 1977. As a classroom teacher at the eighth grade level in the subject area of Earth Science at Rabun County High School, I was well aware that there would be a review conducted by SACS (Southern Association of Colleges and Schools) for the purpose of accreditation.

This is a process of self-study, or evaluation, by the school faculty and staff, concluded with a visiting committee. This group of professional educators would observe the "workings" of our school for three days in the fall of 1977.

Also, the new comprehensive high school, grades 7-12, was being constructed and was due to be ready for occupancy at the beginning of the school term of 1977-1978. Due to delays, the building on the new campus located on Highway 441 South near Tiger was not completely finished.

The decision was made to move into the new facility regardless of the fact that it was incomplete. We teachers and students soon adjusted to the sounds of hammering and earth-moving equipment, and to the voices of the working crews, although "mass chaos and confusion" did occur at times!

During the months of September and October, we school personnel completed the tasks of evaluating all aspects of the school program. This included the areas of instruction, facilities, food service, and defining future goals and objectives.

As the November deadline approached for the visiting committee to arrive, the principal reminded us that during the three days of visitation, a committee member could observe the teaching procedures of any teacher at any time in any building.

He also gave us these instructions: we teachers were to place a chair just inside the classroom, by the door, so that a member of the visiting committee could quietly enter without causing a disturbance. Then the teacher would hand the visitor the lesson plan, course guide, and textbook.

By now the students, from the youngest seventh grader to the mightiest senior, were well aware that "company was a-coming" and the "dog and pony show" was about to begin.

My eighth grade students were involved in a unit on the waters of planet earth; the objective of lesson plan #2 was to gain knowledge of the tides, which is the periodic rise and fall of ocean waters due to the attraction of the sun and the moon. (I felt that this would be a topic of interest as we mountain folk are not very familiar with tides.)

As the second period class was seated on the Monday of visitation, there was a knock on the door. As the neatly dressed man entered, I directed the visitor to the waiting chair and handed him the required materials. He seemed very interested, and I felt very comfortable.

After an introduction on the subject of tides, a film was shown (on a reel-to-reel projector). A class discussion followed. From the textbook, pages 211-215 were read, and assigned seatwork was placed in the science notebook. Instructional aids included examining tide charts, and shell collections by the pupils. Their sea and beach artwork was visible on the bulletin board, and supplementary reading materials were available on all six lab tables.

While every pupil was "on task", I moved over towards the visitor, introduced myself and welcomed him to our school. At this time he stood up, handed back to me the stack of materials and said, "Lady, I have really enjoyed being in your class and learning about the ocean tides, but since I am the Plumbing Engineer for a final walk-through, just let me check the lab sinks in this area, and I'll be on my way!"

After inspecting the waterworks and as he turned to leave, he said to me, "Lady, if I have time, I'll be back for last period class."

Imagine my dismay when I realized he was not a member of the visiting committee – but I daresay he was the most knowledgeable plumber on ocean tides!

The visiting committee made their final report. Eventually the faculty and staff received notice that standards were in compliance; objectives had been met; with only two recommendations to be completed, and Rabun County High School continued to be fully accredited by SACS!

---

# Chapter 7
## Holidays

# The Halloween Cake

I was six years of age and in the first grade at the old Tiger schoolhouse when my mother was elected president of the P.T.A. Immediately, her goal was to provide curtains for the stage in the school auditorium so that the students could enjoy musical performances, plays, and recitations. The fact that the GREAT DEPRESSION made money scarce did not deter the determination of my Mama!!

The annual Halloween Carnival was the first opportunity to raise the necessary funds for this visionary project of securing the stage curtains. For young and old, the Cake Walk was the favorite activity at the carnival. Homemade cakes were baked, decorated, and donated by the ladies of the community, and displayed as prizes for the winners of the Cake Walk.

Halloween, Oct. 31, finally arrived and off to the "fun and games" I went. Immediately, I spotted the most beautiful cake with five chocolate layers, luscious filling, and covered with deep dark chocolate icing. This cake would be awarded to a winner in the Cake Walk.

My own funds were very limited; however, with one of my nickels I joined in the Cake Walk. As the music played, we marched round and round. When the music ceased, I stood on the lucky number, and the heavenly chocolate cake was mine! Then Mama took me behind the piano. She said for me to give the cake back so it could be "walked off" again for more funds for the stage curtains. So I did.

Soon, I spent another nickel to join in the cake walk. Lo and behold, I again was standing on the lucky number! For the second time, the luscious chocolate cake was mine. Once again, Mama whispered to me that the need for the stage curtains was so great that the welfare of the Tiger school and community depended on my giving the cake back as a prize. Reluctantly, I donated it.

As the final Cake Walk began, I spent my remaining nickel to march to the music. The elegant chocolate cake was the last prize. Glory be! I won the cake for the third time! Now the crowd at the Halloween Carnival chanted, "Let her keep it! Let her keep the chocolate cake!" I carefully carried the choice prize cake home, and at Sunday dinner everyone enjoyed sharing the tasty desert, the chocolate cake I had won three times.

# Thanks for the Grands

Thanksgiving season has arrived! Counting among my many blessings, I am truly thankful for my grandchildren. Each is so different, yet so similar. Using the beginning letters of the word Thanksgiving, let me tell you about each. (Remember the old saying that "every Momma Blackbird thinks her baby Blackbird is the blackest". I'm sure that's the way I am about my grands.)

T is for ten, which is a magic number because I have ten grandchildren. I recall the old saying, "There ain't nary a cull in the bunch!"

H is for handsome, which describes Blake Christopher Scott (April 14th, 1979). He graduated from East Hall High School, attended Gainesville College, and is currently employed in the trucking industry. Blake is a most caring and dedicated young man; his loyal companion is a white German Shepherd named Belle.

A is for Arren (a shortened version of the Arrendale family name) Daniel Taylor (December 12, 1999), who is my youngest grandson. At age eight, he is a typical third-grader with an impish smile and bright eyes behind the thick lenses of his glasses. Arren has great athletic ability--he can "run as fast as lightning".

N is for the natural talent of Beau Taylor Bryan (July 30th, 1984). His talented fingers and hands have made award-winning piano music over the years. Beau Taylor, who is named for Big Melvin, is currently enrolled at the Medical College of Georgia, and the same skilled fingers and hands will bring comfort and healing to his patients. He and his wife, the former Catharine Solms, live in Augusta.

K is for Kelli LeAnn Scott (July 6, 1982). A graduate of the University of Georgia, with a Masters degree from Appalachian State College. She is a Research Analyst at North Georgia College and State University. Not only does Kelli have a brilliant mind, she has the features of a fashion model. As the old folks would say, "She's prettier than a speckled pup under a red wagon."

S is for the slender and vivacious Whitney Ellen Ray Cox. (September 17, 1980). Whitney is my oldest granddaughter who has a beautiful, radiant smile. Tall and willowy, she is pretty on the inside and out, and she possesses a deep compassion for others. Whitney is a graduate of Clemson University and is a former kindergarten teacher. Like her brothers and parents, she is a huge sports fan who is currently a stay-at-home mom. Whitney and her husband, Leland, are the parents of two adorable sons, Preston, 3, and Parker, 1.

G is for the Georgia Bulldog fan and ardent supporter, Brooks Patton Ray (April 14, 1976). He is the oldest of my grands, as he was born three minutes ahead of his twin brother Vince! Brooks is a good-looking, caring middle school teacher and coach in Habersham County who holds a Masters degree in Physical Education. Having been involved in athletics all his life, he continues to be an avid sports fan who enjoys fishing and golf as well as following the Georgia Bulldogs. Brooks, along with his twin brother Vince, is a well-mannered Southern gentleman. Brooks and his wife, the former Katie Bowman, are the parents of a beautiful six month old baby girl, Kaleigh Rebecca.

I is for the intelligence of Zackary Cleveland Bryan (October 16, 1977), who is a professional civil engineer, finishing his studies at the University of Georgia in 2000. A fourth-generation surveyor, his office displays (along with the hunting and fishing trophies) the old surveying equipment (compass and steel chain) which he inherited from his great-grandfather, John V. Arrendale, who served many terms as Rabun County's surveyor. Zack is a most-eligible bachelor who lives near Clarkesville.

V is for Vincent Michael Ray (April 14, 1976), who is tall, dark, and good-looking! He is remembered as an outstanding basketball player for both Habersham Central High School and North Georgia State University. Having graduated from Mercer School of Law, he is a practicing attorney. He and his wife, the former Shelley Cox, live in Cumming with their precious son V. J.

I is for the imaginative and creative ability of John Rennard "Renn" Taylor (June 4, 1998), who is now ten years of age. Renn has learned about crops and farming from his Grandpa Melvin. Early on, Renn learned the "tools of the trade" in designing and constructing homes from his dad, Wesley. In a kindergarten activity where students were asked to draw a house, the teacher realized that Renn was spending much more time and effort on the task than others. The others had drawn a simple house. The teacher was amazed to find that, to Renn, "drawing a house" meant a detailed blueprint.

N is for the name: Cameron Leigh Taylor (December 31, 2001) is the youngest granddaughter. At six, she is a fine first grader. Tiny in size with the most expressive blue eyes, Cami learned early from me the art of quilting. She and I were visiting at a "do-up" when she suddenly dropped my hand and loudly announced to all: "Look, Janie P., look! A quilt!" Sure enough, there was a wall hanging of a quilt, in the Log Cabin pattern. Truly, Cami is a "chip off the old block".

G is for the great-grands. Vincent Michael "V.J." Ray (March 22, 2006), John Preston Cox (July 27, 2005), and Michael Parker Cox (July 2, 2007) are the most adorable and precious double-first-cousins. One adorable great-granddaughter, Kaleigh Rebecca Ray (January 27, 2008).

# "One Christmas Tale"

To many of us, Christmas time brings memories of brightly decorated trees surrounded by gifts in holiday wrapping. Not so for my friend, Carol, who recalls a totally different Christmas happening when she was five years old.

Late in the afternoon on Christmas Eve, the mother, Mary, had rushed to town to do some last minute errands. About this time, "Old Buddy" John Melvin (a most eligible bachelor), dropped by to spread Christmas cheer. There was peppermint candy for Carol; and for Papa, a drink of the purest moonshine peach brandy.

When the sound of the car signaling the return home of Mama was heard, Old Buddy panicked. With great haste, he searched for a hiding place for the illicit half-gallon of spirits. When he spotted the washing machine in the kitchen area, he hurriedly placed the mason jar into the tub of the machine. He quickly slammed the door to conceal the forbidden item. Soon, Old Buddy left on his merry way!

You and I know that even on Christmas Eve, it becomes necessary for the mother to wash a load of clothes for the baby. When Mary raised the lid of the washing machine and saw the glass jar of sparkling clear moonshine, she was furious! She grabbed up the detested jar of spirits and placed it inside a large, empty, white shoebox. Then, Mary rushed to the back porch and heaved the box and its contents into the nearby Stekoa Creek. Carol had witnessed all the commotion and watched as the box floated out of sight, carrying its fragile contents on to the Atlantic Ocean.

Amidst the excitement of Christmas morning and the softly falling snowflakes, Old Buddy arrived very early for he was sorely in need of a "toddy" to settle his nerves. Gradually, he moved toward the washing machine to recover his "medicine". Mary, who watched him, announced with great emotion that the half-gallon was in a white shoebox which she threw into the creek and it was long gone.

As Carol followed Old Buddy out to the back porch, she saw him remove his shoes and socks, roll up his pant legs, and jump into the icy waters searching for the white box and its contraband contents. As Carol peered out between the pickets of the back porch railing, she watched as he waded downstream and the snowflakes swirled around. Old Buddy soon spotted the white box caught in an eddy -- a circling current.

Fearing the worst, that the mason jar was broken into a thousand pieces, he gingerly opened the box. Hallelujah!! The glass container had survived the journey floating down the swiftly flowing creek. "A holiday miracle," shouted Old Buddy as he waved the box in the air and climbed out of the freezing water onto the bank.

Many years have passed since this event took place. It is often recalled and has become a traditional tale of every Christmas season.

...................................................................................

## Just What I Wanted for Christmas

On a bright Sunday afternoon in December a few years ago, Melvin and I motored up the highway to visit the new shopping center in east Franklin, North Carolina. With the Christmas gift list in hand, we entered the recently-opened Wal-Mart. Amidst the holiday decorations and tasty goodies, we met friends and some family members, including my sister-in-law, Waunett Sexton, and her husband, Herman.

Later, after we two "Helpers of Santa" loaded the packages into the car's trunk, we settled in for the 29 mile trip back to Tiger Mountain.

As Melvin turned the ignition switch on, the only sound we heard was "CLICK... CLICK... CLICK". He tried again and along with the "CLICK... CLICK..." was a grating sound, as if metal pieces were scraping against each other.

Then Melvin asked, "What is the matter with this car that it won't crank?"

To which I replied, "I've mentioned to you several times that my car was not starting properly!"

"But you didn't tell me it sounded like this," he answered. As my husband got out of the car, he mumbled that women folks didn't know much and even less about automobiles.

Later, after many more "CLICK... CLICK..." sounds, and with no luck using jumper cables nor following the suggestions he got from the gathering crowd of "shade-tree mechanics" and "do-it-yourself-ers" who eventually shook their heads and moved on, the decision was made that my car would have to remain parked at the mall.

Dashing back into the store, Melvin located his kin to "hook a ride" to Tiger. Thanks to these two Christmas angels, we arrived home as the wintry wind turned colder and the evening shadows lengthened.

At 4:00 the next morning I was awakened by Melvin saying, "Get up! We're going to Franklin to bring your car home." Traveling in the glow of the moonlight and shivering in the early morning chill, the "plan" was revealed to me. In the empty parking lot we would push my car, gaining speed up to 35 miles an hour and, hopefully, the engine would crank. As the dawn hours turned into daylight, round and round we traveled, but to no avail. Only more "CLICK... CLICK..."

Melvin decided we would return to Clayton and borrow a set of super-strong jumper cables from a local garage. So, another 29-mile journey each way back to Rabun County, returning immediately to the now-familiar shopping center which was by this time in a frenzy of activity with holiday shoppers, walkers, and coffee drinkers. Songs of the season could be heard and Christmas excitement was in the air.

With the stronger jumper cables in place, Melvin instructed me to get in the driver's seat and, as the motor turned, for me to keep it running and not let it go dead!

As the electrical energy was expended, the car motor started and began humming. The nearby on-lookers whistles and cheered. Then... silence. Total silence except for "CLICK... CLICK...!"

Melvin, in his strong voice, using an old mountain adage, yelled, "Janie P., you cannot drive a stob in a fat hawg's hind-end!" To this the crowd echoed, "No, she can't drive a stob in a fat hawg's hind-end!"

Next the husband said to his wife, "You hold the jumper cables and I will keep this car engine running!" The engine started and as I removed the jumper cables, he shouted, "Honey, pick me up at the corner of the stop light in Clayton."

The crowd clapped and cheered as he drove out of the parking area. Waving his arm, we heard him exclaim as he turned on his way, "Merry Christmas to all — and have a good day!"

Driving his car, I followed my car down Highway 441-15 South. Then, amidst the Christmas decorations of green garlands and twinkling lights, there was Melvin standing on the corner at the red light in Clayton, wearing his red and white knitted cap and chatting with the local Santa Claus. Truly, peace on earth and good will towards his wife had begun!

My Christmas present that season was not a new car – but a new starter for the old one!

# Awry in a Manger

As the Christmas season approached, the church committee decided that once again the annual Nativity scene would be presented by the younger children. As in the past, generations of family members would be present to receive this traditional Christmas blessing.

The Biblical characters were chosen. Renn Taylor was to be Shepherd #1, his brother Arren would be Shepherd #2. The mother of the two boys began preparing the outfits for the Shepherds: coordinated bathrobe outfits in wine and brown colors with matching headpieces and plaited belts. The father carved a staff for each Shepherd. He also took a fishing pole and attached a large, bright star to it, to hang over the manger scene. Too, the father helped construct a sturdy wooden stable for the stage.

The rehearsal went well. There were no speaking parts, and the little ones practiced the singing of "Away in a Manger". However, on the morning of the performance day, two wooden life-size donkeys with long ears were given to the drama department. These two pretend donkeys were moveable, as small rollers were attached to the hooves. Immediately, it was decreed that Shepherd Renn and Shepherd Arren would each lead Donkey #1 and Donkey #2 respectively, onto the stage, as an addition to the Nativity scene.

The Christmas program began. Inside the stable, Mary and Joseph were proudly watching over the Baby Jesus. The little Angels were all a-flutter with sparkling wings and rhinestone tiaras. The Wise Men, dressed in purple and red velvet robes with jeweled turbans, knelt, bearing their gifts. Unfortunately, Shepherd Renn with Donkey #1 and Shepherd Arren with Donkey #2, attempted to enter through the same door at the same time. Amidst much pushing and shoving, the foursome finally took their assigned places. (From the audience, giggles and twittering can be heard.)

Shepherd Renn was having a most difficult time as Donkey #1 was very unsteady, and--oops!--the donkey collapsed to the floor. With brotherly concern, Shepherd Arren tried to assist, but his bathrobe belt became entwined in the wheels of Donkey #2, which had overturned. Both shepherds, with their costumes in total disarray, attempted to right the donkeys, known now as "Stupid" and "Dummy". (From the audience, roars of laughter can be heard.)

The father of the Shepherds slid down into his seat, hands over his face, wishing to remove himself from this disaster. He whispered to his wife, "Mama, can't you do something -- just anything?" To which wife replied, "Me, why me? I never saw those two boys in my life!"

Mass chaos and confusion continued as the fishing pole supporting the star came undone, causing the celestial body to swing aimlessly. Suddenly, Shepherd Arren caught a glimpse of the wayward star. He proceeded to climb up the outside wall of the stable, but he couldn't reach the star. Shepherd Arren climbed down and returned to the area of the fallen donkeys. To observe the goings-on more closely, Mary and Joseph left their assigned positions, standing in an effort to get a clearer picture. The Wise Men are no longer kneeling, but are leaning forward, their gifts in total disarray. The wings of the Angels have drooped; each hides her face in shock and dismay. Through it all, the Baby Jesus slept undisturbed by the commotion. The concern over the instability of the donkeys continued, however. Shepherd Arren spotted his father, seated below him, and hollered, "Dad, make Renn give me back my donkey!" (From the audience, hysterical laughter can be heard. Members of the congregation are bent double, gasping for breath, with tears rolling down their cheeks.)

The curtain closes. Moments later, it opens. All of the cast members are in place, including the two shepherds and their donkeys. The Heavenly Star is brightly shining in its proper place; the musical notes of "Away in a Manger" are heard. (From the audience, the applause is deafening as a standing ovation is given.)

---

123

# Celebrating Christmas Early

The joy and excitement of the holiday season was most evident as family members recently gathered to honor my husband, Melvin Taylor, on his 80th birthday. Instead of the traditional Christmas dinner of turkey and dressing, the 116 kinfolks feasted on barbecue and fixings. The many gifts were wrapped in colorful paper of orange, pink, and purple, not in the Yuletide colors of red and green. No Christmas tree was needed for the mountains glowed with glorious fall foliage. A Christmas-like surprise was a video tribute produced by our son, Wesley Taylor. This presentation included over 300 photographs of "kin and friend", and was truly a pictorial history of several generations of our families.

This will be the first Christmas for our great-grandson, John Preston Cox. At three months of age, he smiled and gurgled as if Santa had already arrived! The oldest person present was my uncle, Dr. Joe Arrendale, who at age 89 recalled earlier birthdays and Christmas "doings". A most honored guest was a first cousin of Melvin's, Annette Moore Garber. Now confined to a wheelchair, and at age 88, she has happy memories of past holidays.

As I began gathering the needed items for the "do-up", I found the CHRISTMAS tablecloth!! Thus a tale to tell:

Fifty years ago, my Mama Clyde traveled to Europe. While in Ireland, she purchased a pure linen, banquet size, white embroidered tablecloth with 12 large matching table napkins. A most treasured possession, this table cover was rarely used except at Christmas.

Mama Clyde had a beloved milk cow named Beauty, who was of the Jersey breed and literally produced gallons of milk daily! However, Beauty had a "failing", she had the ability to get out of the pasture by jumping over or crawling under any fence.

As Christmas approached, Mama Clyde had carefully washed the fragile Irish linen tablecloth. As the day was clear and crisp, she hung her prized item on the outside clothesline to dry as it gently billowed and waved in the breeze. All of this caught the attention of Beauty, who immediately conquered the pasture fence and happily began chewing, slobbering, and enjoying the "flavor" of the tablecloth. Eventually, Mama Clyde discovered the wayward cow and by hollering and yelling managed to salvage the cloth. (Any other cow would have been hauled off to market, but not Beauty!) Mama patiently patched, darned, and labored to repair the damage by Christmas 1955, and this same cloth was used at the "big do-up" on Melvin's birthday. Today the 12 matching linen dinner napkins are proudly used as mantel-shelf scarves in the nearly new home of my sister, Peggy, as she decorates for Christmas.

To all of you, dear Readers, who celebrate birthdays at Christmas time, I wish for you a happy day! Just like the one we had for Melvin Taylor!

One of my great-grandmothers was born on December 25 -- a Christmas Gift! The baby was given the name of Mary (for Merry) Christmas Gupton. As her name indicated, Mary brought much joy and happiness to her family and friends. I've been told that she always had a smile and a kind word for one and all. At age 16, Mary embroidered a linen sampler, which I have hanging above my desk today. It reads, "Let not your heart be troubled". Truly, this was Grandmother Mary's motto for her life as she radiated love and acceptance.

Strangely enough, Grandmother Mary died, also on December 25, Christmas Day. Her grave site is located in the family plot surrounded by an iron picket fence. Her cemetery monument in this peaceful final resting place reads: Mary (Merry) Christmas Gupton -- Born December 25, 1859, Died December 25, 1918.

At the top of the marble tombstone there is a skillful carving, a work of art -- a perfect Christmas Rose!

---

# Melvin Taylor's Christmas in China

Stationed in faraway China with the U.S. occupational forces, following the surrender of Japan, Melvin Taylor was not anticipating a happy holiday season. Being away from home and family and in a different country, Melvin and his fellow marines were a bit homesick! Morale was low.

After arriving in Tieutsin, China, Melvin and the troops hired two Chinese men to assist with housekeeping duties and daily tasks. The older man was called "Ole Joe", and his son-in-law was "Lu". For their work, the two were paid top wages in American money at 65 cents per week. Early on a particular Christmas morning, "Lu" arrived as usual, but "Ole Joe" was absent. Fearing that "Ole Joe" was ill or injured, Melvin questioned "Lu", who simply mumbled an answer in Chinese. Now, the guys had another worry: "Where was 'Ole Joe?'"

Suddenly, "Lu" began shouting and pointing down the road. "Ole Joe" was in view, but splashes of red and green were also visible! As "Ole Joe" approached, the marines saw that "Ole Joe" had a long pole across his aging shoulders. Suspended from the pole were ten flower pots filled with massive poinsettias in full bloom, with rich red leaf-like flowers and brilliant green foliage. "Ole Joe" had walked nine miles carrying these Christmas gifts for his American friends.

The combat-hardened leathernecks cheered and clapped on "Ole Joe" and the never-to-be forgotten presents of poinsettia. The spirit of Christmas had returned.

---

# A Valentine Tale
## Grandpa Mart's Mail-Order Bride

Valentine's Day is a celebration of love that comes in many shapes, forms, and fashions. On this particular Valentine's Day, February 14th in 1932, my great-grandfather, Martin L. Arrendale, was dressed up in his Sunday best. He was a tall, handsome and intelligent man of 73 years who was a widower, having previously buried two wives. Grandpa Mart then disclosed that he was motoring down to the train depot in Cornelia to meet his new wife! Grandpa Mart had answered an advertisement in the weekly paper, *The Market Bulletin*, for a mail-order bride. Consequently, sight unseen, he mailed to Bertha Faye an offer of marriage and a train ticket for transportation from her home in South Georgia to these northeastern highlands.

When the train pulled into the station, an attractive, middle-aged, healthy spinster disembarked and Grandpa Mart's new companion had arrived! Straight to the Habersham Courthouse the two went, and the judge pronounced them husband and wife. Bertha Faye and Grandpa Mart returned to his home on Bridge Creek, and he immediately sent word for his shocked and surprised children (and their grandchildren!) to come visit and greet Bertha Faye on the following Sunday.

The day was pleasant enough, and the Valentine arrow from Cupid had hit its mark! Unfortunately, this Valentine love affair was not a "marriage made in heaven" nor does this story have a happy ending. Bertha Faye had discovered that inside the corn crib was a jug of mountain "corn-squeezings", commonly known as 190 proof moonshine whiskey. She made regular trips down the path to the corn crib and soon became very much at ease in her new surroundings! On Monday, Bertha Faye was visibly "under the influence", and by Tuesday, she was highly inebriated. In a state of drunkenness on Wednesday, Bertha Faye built a roaring fire under the large black wash pot in the backyard. She went into the smoke house and selected the largest cured ham. Staggering, Bertha threw the whole ham into the boiling water and hollered, "I believe in having plenty!" This tale occurred during the Great Depression when food was a scarce commodity. Grandpa Mart was also a frugal mountaineer who believed in "waste not, want not" and to cook an entire ham was unthinkable!

Grandpa Mart held his tongue and temper at the sight of his cooked (whole) ham and intoxicated wife, but his piercing steel blue eyes revealed his dismay and disgust. Grandpa Mart was now aware that his mail-order bride had a severe drinking problem and an uncontrollable addiction to alcohol. Calmly Grandpa Mart instructed Bertha Faye to pack her belongings. The silent Valentine couple traveled to the depot in Tiger for Bertha Faye to catch the southbound afternoon train; not unexpectedly, the train ticket that delivered her home to her kinfolks in the South Georgia flatlands was one-way.

After a quiet divorce, Grandpa Mart never again mentioned the episode of the Valentine mail-order bride. His last years at the old home place were content where he lived near his daughter Lizzie.

For years Grandpa Mart operated the community grist mill.

# MO-THER Tales

Over the years, my children have referred to me as Mama, mom- or even Janie P. However, when I am called Mo-ther, I know that a crisis has occurred or that I am in BIG trouble! On St. Patrick's Day, my grandson, Renn, spent the afternoon with me at Tiger. On hand, I had several cupcakes with multicolored frosting to celebrate the March 18th birthday of St. Paddy. The abundant amount of fluffy sweet icing was most colorful. Renn and I did finger-painting with the goo in shades of red, yellow, blue, and most definitely, green. He and I enjoyed licking our fingers and tasting yummy bite after bite.

Early the next morning, I received a telephone call. "MO-THER," asked my son Wesley, "Do you know anything about what Renn ate at your house yesterday?" I quickly answered that Renn enjoyed beans and corn bread and we also ate the St. Patrick's Day cupcakes with icing of many tones and hues. To this, Wesley replied, "Thank goodness! Renn has just had a psychedelic colored BM, and the toilet bowl is filled with brilliant green water with miniature rainbows floating about!" With a sigh of relief, he said, " Have a good day and bye, Mama."

\* \* \* \* \*

While traveling towards home on a windy March day with Wesley, Karen, and Renn, we stopped for a late lunch at a well-known "eating joint" near Atlanta. As we finished the meal, Renn and I observed an accumulation of pork rib bones. Immediately, we thought of the beloved black cocker spaniel named Burnt Toast (or B.T.) who deserved these tasty morsels. Since Wesley never, ever approves of my requesting a Doggie Bag, nor a treat for a pet sack, I decided to secretly salvage the bones. Wrapping the collection in paper napkins, I hid them in my pocketbook. Once inside the SUV, I slid the contraband items under the front seat.

A few days later the telephone rang. When I answered, I heard the dreaded sound of "MO-THER." Wesley questioned me, "Do you know anything about a batch of dog scraps stuffed under the car seat?" (Instantly, I recalled that I had not removed the special treats for B.T.) The call continued, "MO-THER! The putrid smell of decaying meat is terrible and the stench unbearable!" Humbled, but what could I say except that "I'm sorry"? I offered to write a check to cover the deodorizing of the van. Laughingly, Wesley said, "You are forgiven. Have a good day. Bye, Mama."

\* \* \* \* \*

One morning in March, Wesley called, "MO-THER, Renn is sick can you come spend a day with him?" So, I motored down the road. Renn and I read books, played games, watched videos, and ate numerous snacks. Next, we decided to play "beauty parlor" and Renn, at age five, would give me a manicure and pedicure. We selected the most vivid red nail color and he polished my ten fingernails and began to paint my toenails. Unfortunately, but not unexpectedly, the bottle of polish tipped over. I quickly grabbed the nearest cloth (which was a fancy linen guest towel) and began wiping up the red spill. I was thinking that a bit of nail polish remover would eliminate the evidence but I forgot to finish the task.

The telephone call came the next morning. "MO-THER, Do you know anything about the nail polish smeared on the guest towel and drops of bright red on the floor and the vanity of the powder room?" I began to account for "the cause and effect" of such happenings. Without further comments, Wesley soothed my feelings by stating "Don't worry about it! Have a good day. Bye, Mama"

Janie P. with grandson, Renn Taylor

# Mother's Day Ruby Reminder

Sunday, May 12th, is Mother's Day. It also happens to be the 43rd wedding anniversary for Melvin and me. It began when we drove to Walhalla, South Carolina, for a civil marriage ceremony, and Melvin put a wide gold wedding band on the third finger of my left hand. Getting married in Walhalla has always been a tradition around these parts.

Six years later, again on Mother's Day and our anniversary, Melvin handed me a small square box. Nestled inside on the velvet lining was a ring with an oval, brilliant red stone. This small circle of metal and mineral, fit the third finger of my right hand perfectly! The gem stone appeared to be a ruby or corundum, with a "visible star" deep within. The radiating points from the rich-red center were indicative of a precious ruby. Melvin gave an account of the history of my gift.

While serving with the U.S. Marines on the mainland of China in 1945, an elderly ragged street person approached and offered this ring for sale. Melvin bought it for $3.00 in American money. The boxed ring had been forgotten amidst other belongings and mementos of his days in service. Gazing into the stone, I began to wonder. Had this treasure once belonged to a Czarina of Russia? And, had the ring traveled over tundra, forests, fertile plains, and deserts to eventually find its way into the hands of the aged China man? Or, perhaps it was a stolen jewel from the collection of an Empress of China which had washed down the Yellow River, was discovered and placed into the ring box to be traded. Those secrets of my ring will never be known!

Twelve years later, I decided to include the ring in an insurance policy and was required to have an appraisal. So we consulted professional jewelers in Atlanta. They informed me that the stone demonstrated the qualities of a true ruby but would have to go to New York City for expert examination. I could not agree to this. The only detail that caused a question was that the stone was set in silver which is uncharacteristic of jewelers due to the softness of the ring settings. The jeweler told me that regardless, if the stone was a valuable ruby or a perfect synthetic gemstone that it should be worn every day and never placed in a safety box. After all, who would believe I was wearing a ruby? So, I couldn't get the appraisal to insure it and chose to wear it every day.

Once, after shelling a bushel of field peas to freeze, I realized that my ring was missing. To my relief, a neighbor with his metal detecter located the ring in the mass of pea hulls. And another time, the ring fell and bounced into the depths of the central heating system, and a most sympathetic technician retrieved it for hysterical me! The beauty of this gift has brought me great joy and has added a deep history from Tiger to the mystery of my Mother's Day and anniversary ruby.

..............................................................................................

## Dedicated to Great-Grandmothers Everywhere

Many people never have the opportunity to know and love their great-grandmothers. As Mother's Day approaches, I have found myself recalling the wonderful times I spent with my great-grandmother, Tallulah Ellen Edwards Arrendale. Although she suffered from dementia the last decade of her life, my visits with her gave me insight into the long, productive life she lived.

Spending time with her allowed me to catch glimpses of the strong woman she was and had always been. Grandma Arrendale was a woman of character, graciousness, and faith.

One of my earliest memories of Grandma was sitting with her at a card table playing a game of Scrabble. My maternal grandmother, Clyde Ellen Arrendale English, her daughter, was with us as was often the case. So, there I sat, sandwiched between two brilliant minds, and they were treating me as an equal. As a young child, I was very impressed!

The game progressed, and it was my turn. Grandma and MaClyde waited patiently and assured me there was no rush. Finally, after much thought, I placed my tiles on the game board to complete my turn. Grandma and MaClyde nodded with approval and praised my efforts. Now, they didn't overdo the accolades because it was taken for granted that I could reason and spell since I came from good stock and was born with "plenty of sense"! (After all, my grandmother and her siblings all had advanced college degrees as does my mother and her siblings. My generation had to follow suit.)

Along with the games of Scrabble, we always had refreshments or what we called "tea parties". Ever the lovely hostess, Grandma served me hot tea or coffee, which was mostly milk in a pretty china cup and saucer. Next she passed around a plate of her soft, homemade sugar cookies. (After her death we searched diligently for a written recipe with no luck. Believe me, those cookies can't be duplicated!)

How grown up I felt as we resumed our board game! If possible, a game started led to a game finished. As well, rules were rules, and they were strictly adhered to by all players. There were no gray areas with Grandma — integrity and honesty were expected in a game of Scrabble as well as in the games of life!

Grandma was a wonderful hostess in every way. Family and friends were always welcome in her home and around her table. She enjoyed setting a beautiful table, complete with linen tablecloth, matching napkins, and untarnished silverware. She was a role model to all her descendants in proper mealtime etiquette. She expected us to be on our best behavior with our table manners intact when we shared a meal together. There never was any pretentiousness about Grandma — she simply exuded the highest level of common courtesy along with a healthy dose of common sense. She was a marvelous cook and folks never left her home hungry.

As a teenager, many a Sunday morning found me at Grandma's house in order for the hired caretaker to have the day off. I unofficially became Grandma's "lady-in-waiting". It was great fun for me to style her hair and give her a manicure. Also, I helped her choose her dress for the day. I assisted her in putting on the dress only after I helped her with the proper undergarments. (She always wore a full slip and stockings; after all, she had been "raised right" in the old Deep South!)

Then together we would look through the contents of her jewelry box to find the perfect adornment for her dress. More often than not she chose a brooch rather than a necklace. As finishing touches, I brightened her face with a little rouge and powder and dabbed perfume behind her ears.

Grandma was a woman of high moral principles, and it showed even in her attire and in the way she presented herself. Modesty and respectability were second nature to her.

Grandma was a devout Christian lady who practiced what she preached. She shared her faith by example. Many times when I walked into her house to visit, I would find her in her chair next to the window reading her Bible. She was well-versed in the Scriptures since she had read the Good Book from beginning to end countless times. She was a staunch Methodist who took the fourth commandment very seriously.

To her, Sunday was a day of rest, reflection, and renewal following Sunday School and preaching. No work was allowed by Grandma on the Sabbath. Grandma lived what she believed, and she exemplified all the traits of a godly woman.

Shortly after her 85th birthday, she wrote my Aunt Peggy the following: *Really and truly, my life has fallen in pleasant places, and I have a goodly heritage. Each of our children are helpful citizens and upright leading members of their own communities and are helping this world to be a better place to live, so what more can a mother or grandmother ask? The Lord has been good to me.*

This Mother's Day, I will continue to remind myself of my rich family heritage, and I will celebrate the fact that I am a link in a chain of strong, wonderful women who have contributed to the person I am today. I will always be Grandma Arrendale's great-granddaughter, MaClyde's granddaughter, Janie P.'s daughter, Lucy's cousin, Aunt Peggy's niece, Judy and Dawne's sister, Whitney Ellen Cox's mother and Kaleigh Rebecca Ray's grandmother.

May I be faithful in continuing to pass along the wisdom, traditions, and blessings that were passed down to me.

by Janie P. Taylor with Daughter Becky Ray

## Biography
### Tallulah "Lula" Ellen Edwards Arrendale

Tallulah "Lula" Ellen Edwards began her life on this earth on January 17, 1878. The daughter of Cinderella Ann Hanson Edwards and John C. Edwards, she was born in Starr, near Forsyth, Georgia. Later, Dublin became home until she attended the State Normal School, now the Education College of the University of Georgia. Upon graduation, she came to Rabun Gap Industrial School as the domestic science teacher and met Jon V. Arrendale. They married in June 1906. While raising their four children, she was postmistress at Tiger and assisted in the poultry industry in this area. During the Depression, the Arrendales moved to Athens, so their children could live at home while attending the University of Georgia. She supplemented the family income by running a boarding house during this time. She participated in many community and church activities throughout her life. She passed to her Eternal Home on March 10, 1973, at the age of 95 and is buried in the Tiger Cemetery alongside her husband.

# Chapter 8
# Memories

# These walls talk, just stop and listen

by Linda Angel

In starting to write this article, I first paid a visit to Janie P. Taylor to get the information. She had quotes from her kids and grandkids, because they have so many special memories of their Mama Clyde and her home. There was so much information that I decided to use their stories and quotes instead of writing mine.

It is an honor for me to write this story, because Mrs. Pleasants (as I called her) was a great part of my life, also. She was my teacher in elementary school and was always encouraging and understanding. She recognized my love for books and was most helpful in forming my reading habits. Today, my favorite hobby is still reading.

On a gentle knoll in Tiger, sits a small white house that you would think might need to be the size of the Coliseum to hold all the memories from the life and times of Clyde Ellen Arrendale Pleasants English. It started out as a very small log house. The log portion of the house was built in 1825 and is still a part of the structure. A new part was added in 1909 and another in 1940, which had to be torn down. A very attractive addition stands in its place—built with a lot of the old wood and beams from the old structure.

MaClyde's grandson, Wesley Taylor, inherited the home. His goal was to restore the home, bringing it up to date. He has done an amazing job of adding the modern conveniences (heat and air, kitchen appliances, and wonderfully tiled bathrooms) to the home. He has kept the old pine floors in some rooms, kept an original fireplace and used stone from another fireplace to build one in the new addition. Some of the log walls are left exposed to add to the atmosphere of the home.

Perhaps the most interesting feature in the home are the gun ports in the wall on the stairway. They are a part of the original home and were used to watch and protect the family from raiding Cherokee Indians.

The stories and quotes that follow are from Mama Clyde's family. I think they express the story of this home better than anyone else could!

Jim Pleasants, Son

How Old Is Mama's House?

When I was growing up, the stories all were, "This house is over 100 years old". Since that was in the 1940's, that would put the construction of the house well earlier than 1840, but how much earlier?

Rabun County was formed December 21, 1819. Any resident who was not an Indian would have been a squatter, so there is little likelihood that a permanent house was in existence before the county was surveyed in 1820 and the Land Lottery of 1820 distributed the land. Building a permanent structure before the land titles were settled would have been risky. So, we can be reassured that the earliest possible time for construction was 1820.

The earliest transaction which I have found for the land was the deed from Wm. Jones to John Keener on July 2, 1835. I suspect the house was standing at the time, because the price was high for unimproved property.

I have concluded that the house was built about 1825.


Peggy Pleasants Thrasher, Daughter

My brother, Jim and I were born, delivered by Dr. J.C. Dover, in this house. We also had the pleasure of being raised there. We did not realize that we were "children of Appalachia" as we had such a great place in which to grow up!

During the last half of the century, this home was a gathering place for family, friends, and neighbors. As kids we played in the meadows, woods, and creeks and learned at our Mother's knees of the wonders of nature.

Many of her students recall the sleep-overs at Mama Clyde's house. They, too, treasure memories of the old log house, and it was a valuable learning experience.

In 1959, Mama hosted the lovely wedding reception for Albert and me in her home. She loved having company and Mama's hospitable expression was "The latchstring is always out". We enjoyed myriad family feeds, birthday dinners, feeding local pastors and their families and many social events. Perhaps her favorites were the quilting bees. These were made simple by having the quilting frames suspended from the ceiling and could be lowered on a moments notice!

And, yes, this home has seen many sad gatherings after funerals. It has afforded much comfort to many.

Wesley Taylor, Grandson

"One of my first memories is walking from my house up the hill to MaClyde's house. As I grew up, I learned from her of the old customs of these mountains, like making lye soap, churning and making butter, and to "put up" a quilt. Most of all, I learned to have a genuine appreciation for my family, nature, and my heritage." Wesley also attributes this appreciation to his parents and to Foxfire.

The home place was deeded to me after the death of MaClyde in 1999.

Remembering all she taught me during my childhood, "my growing-up" years, and as an adult grandson, I have commenced to remodel, restore and make historically livable, this treasured dwelling. So, to have this home place to celebrate her life is of great importance to me!

_____

The Annual Arrendale Family Reunion is being held at "Mama's House" on the second Saturday in June. Mama would be proud.

# Tree and Janie P.

For the past one hundred and eighty one years, the white house on the hill has overlooked the valley below. Standing as a sentinel is the massive black walnut tree. Both of these "old timers" are located near Tiger Mountain and each has observed "lots of living a-going on". Thus a story:

As I walked up the rock steps to the front porch at Mama's house, I heard the slight movement of the tiny green leaves of the walnut tree. Then I heard a whisper, " What is going on with the home place, Janie P.? I need an update."

"Tree," I replied, "The original log house is being restored with strong steel underpinnings to support the structure. Additions, from over the years, have been removed, and all materials that are usable have been saved. A new back room is now being built, for more space, and to stabilize the log house."

Tree pondered these words, and then stated, "I was just a sapling when the neighbors gathered for a house raising and chimney building for an early settler, Mr. John Keener, who lived here for 53 years with his beloved wife Elizabeth."

"Tree," I continued, "You were a seedling in 1819 when this area was ceded to the State of Georgia by a treaty with the Cherokee. Then, these mountain lands were distributed by a lottery, or drawing, for land lots. Veterans from the Revolutionary War and the War of 1812 received acreage for their service. My great-great-great grandfather, Thomas Arrendale, was the first settler in the Burton Community in what became the county of Rabun. A neighbor and friend of his was Gold Tooth Tom, a Cherokee who had served as a guide with the Colonial Militia as these troops defeated British Redcoats."

"Prior to 1840," Tree said, "there was a need for portholes in the outside wall of the stairwells. These 2" by 5" rectangular openings were used as spaces for the flint lock rifles to protect the pioneers from attack by Indian war parties. Around 1855, bubbly glass panes were installed where the glow of the lamp light was visible.

"By 1909, a kitchen-dining room was added to the back. Building materials from an abandoned cabin, similar to the wood in the log house, was used. These Scot-Irish settlers wasted nothing. A second chimney was built from soapstone cut out with a cross-cut saw from the quarry near the Arrendale home place. These blocks of rock were brought over here in a sled pulled by a team of oxen," Tree mentioned, "A heavy load indeed!"

"In the 20s, hard times were at hand," Tree remembered, "During the Great Depression, you and your family came here to stay."

"Tree," I asked, " do you recall my finding the U.S. stamp dated 1840 when a doorway was cut through the log wall into the new kitchen area?"

The answer was, "Yes, yes, yes."

"I remember too when the hand-dug well was replaced with a supply from a clear spring through a system of pipes into the house by the power of gravity." Tree mused, " Modernized plumbing had arrived!"

Tree asked, "Is that footed bath tub, I watched being unloaded, still in use?"

To this I replied, "Yes, but as we speak, the tub is being re-glazed and will be placed in the new bathroom being added."

"Wiring for electric power was installed when I was five years old, but the main source of heat was the fireplace for many decades. After World War II, the two dormer windows were added, and the large loft (with hand-hewn wide floor planks) was divided into bedrooms and closet storage space." I recalled.

"Now, Janie P." said Tree. "Do me one big favor, or last request, if I may."

"Yes Tree, what is it?" I questioned.

Tree answered, "My limbs are beginning to weaken and break off, and someday I will be felled by either the wind or an axe. Just pass the word to the next generations that my trunk be made into long boards for a sturdy "eating table" of my black walnut wood. This is to be placed INSIDE the house that I have guarded from the OUTSIDE for lo these many years."

"Tree, I promise to pass the word onto Renn, Arren, V.J. and Preston," I stated. With a tiny rustle of the leaves, Tree was speaking no more, and I felt a soft breeze. Teary-eyed, I realized that the conversation was over once and for all!

# Remembering Two Tiger Ladies
## Lula and Lizzie

From 1913-1917 my grandmother, Tallulah E. "Lula" Arrendale, was postmistress of the Tiger Post Office. Working with her was a rural mail carrier who traveled by horseback and delivered the mail every third day. As the years went by, the Tiger route increased in mileage as portions of Lake Burton, Seed Lake, and Lake Rabun were added. Eventually, the Tiger RFD grew to be the longest mail route in the United States.

When I traveled off to college, I was immediately asked, "Where are you from?" To this, I replied, "I live three miles down the road from Clayton." Then my new friend exclaimed, "You are from Tiger!" I realized that because so many people have second homes in this area with a Tiger address, it is a most recognized place. Never again did I hesitate to say that Tiger is my home!

In the 1970's, the popular television show, Hee Haw, saluted the city of Tiger. Yes, "Sa-lute! Tiger, Georgia, population 189" was heard across the nation and even on the Armed Forces Network. Was Tiger spotlighted on Hee Haw because of its unusual name or was Tiger recognized because the late Junior Samples, star of Hee Haw, reportedly purchased his "spirits" locally? Anyway, just recalling this happening makes the 100th Celebration of Tiger even more exciting! SA-LUTE. Tiger, it's your birthday!

As a child in Tiger we used to gather (other Tiger children) and make for the rock cliffs of Tiger Mountain. We'd explore and travel to the level spot on top. If we carefully timed our trip, we could watch the locomotive and rail cars on the Tallulah Falls railroad tracks approach the Tiger Station. We would watch to see puffs of white "smoke" escape from the whistle of the engine; and then wait and listen quietly, for several seconds, to hear the "Toot Toot" sound of the whistle. From this, we learned early a practical application of the science principle that the speed of light waves is thousands of times faster than the speed of sound vibrations.

Lizzie Keason remembered...

Mrs. Lizzie Keason, the beloved midwife, community leader, and faithful trustee of the Tiger Methodist Church, had three old fashioned clocks standing on the fireplace mantle in her mountain home in Tiger. However, the three clocks did not keep the same time; nor did they strike in accord. For instance, at noon time, each clock would chime twelve times but at different intervals.

So, one day I asked Mrs. Keason about the different readings of the three clocks on the mantelpiece. To my question, she replied, "The first clock on the left side tells "radio time", the middle clock shows "train time", and the other keeps "sun time"." Next, I asked how, with three differing clock readings, did she know what time to go to Sunday morning "Preaching" service. To this her answer was, "Why, I go whenever I get myself ready!" Since Mrs. Keason was never late for church, I knew then that her own "internal clock" was the one that counted -- not the mantel timepieces.

---

Tallulah E. "Lula" Arrendale

Mrs. Lizzie Keason

# A Tribute to the Littlest Hero

Families are joined in love by the sharing of events and by the recalling of memorable times. This happening took place on Germany Mountain Road in Rabun County on Tuesday, September 25, 1934, 72 years ago.

At mid-morning, Leamon Taylor and his wife, Minnie Whitmire Taylor, decided to go to town. With them were their two younger sons, James Hoyt, who was age four, and Denver Victor, age two. The oldest boys, John Melvin and Rennard Ervin, were at school.

As the family motored along the narrow unpaved dirt road, the pickup truck veered off the road and overturned into a nearby ravine. Mr. Leamon and Mrs. Minnie, with Denver in his mother's lap, were pinned under the vehicle. Within seconds, little Hoyt was able to climb out of the cab, unhurt, but very frightened. Then Mr. Leamon said to the four-year-old, "Go get help for us, Hoyt. Run down the road to the first house." When the youngster hesitated, his dad said, "Go son, and hurry!," as the smell of the leaking gasoline was very strong. The courageous little mountain boy, who had been taught to mind his elders, began running barefoot as fast as his little legs could carry him. Down the road and up the a hill, Hoyt ran glancing back at the silent wreck scene. Only the chirping of the birds could be heard. Over the steep hill and around the next curve, Hoyt saw the home of Molly and John McCurry. Out of breath from running so fast, and stammering with fright and anxiety, the McCurrys could not understand his frantic message. Hoyt then took the hand of John McCurry, pulled on his coat sleeve, and led him to the road. As the two raced to the wreck, the seriousness of the situation was most evident as the smell of gasoline vapors was stronger now. John McCurry knew that the slightest spark would ignite the fumes and that an explosion would be a terrible tragedy.

As Mr. Leamon was removed from beneath the car, Hoyt rushed into the arms of his dad, and the two clung together. They watched as the badly injured wife and mother was rescued from the wreckage; she smiled and waved weakly at the father and son. Then sad news was heard that the baby boy, Denver, was not breathing and had been killed by a fatal injury (a broken neck) at the instant of impact. Hoyt, who had been watching and listening, suddenly began softly crying against the shoulder of Mr. Leamon and asked, "Daddy, if I had run faster and got help here quicker, would Denver be able to go play with me?" To this his father replied, "No, my son, you did all you could do by running for help. You are a brave boy."

By now, Aunt Nora Taylor Garland had arrived. Hugging the child close to her heart, she said, "Come along home with me, Hoyt. We'll eat dinner and you can take a nap." Hand in hand, the littlest hero and his auntie went on their way.

Hoyt grew up to be a handsome and likable man. He joined the Navy and lived in California for many years, finally returning home to Rabun. Today, Hoyt lies in rest at the Wolfork Baptist Church Cemetery near the grave of his little brother Denver and close to the graves of his beloved mother and father, who Hoyt saved from an early fiery death on that September day long ago.

Years ago, Hoyt brought to me a basket of jonquil bulbs which he had dug up from the homeplace. These are my "Hoyt" flowers; and as the yellow blooms sway in the breeze, I am reminded of the tow-headed youngster of age four who saved his Ma and Pa from early death by running a half-mile to get aid.

---

Hoyt Taylor

# Getting Around in Rabun County

The first two automobiles owned in Rabun County were a 1915 Buick belonging to Dr. J. C. Dover and a 1917 Ford, property of my Grandaddy Arrendale. The old wagon trails were the only roads and the conditions for traveling by car were deplorable at best.

One wet wintery day, Grandaddy went to Warwoman to check some sick cattle and was returning towards Tiger when he met the other "horseless carriage". Dr. Dover was going to make a house call below the dell. When the two vehicles met on the same narrow curve, one traveling east and the other west, neither driver would budge! Since stubbornness was a male mountaineer trait, neither one nor the other would relinquish the right of way. So the first wreck or collision occurred! As far as we can tell, this was the first motor vehicle accident recorded in our local history. And so it was...

Along the lines of transportation history in Rabun County, The Tallulah Falls Railroad, with a route from Cornelia, Georgia to Franklin, North Carolina, would occasionally derail or have a minor collision. At such times, the stationmaster would notify the home office in Richmond, Virginia by telegraphing a lengthy report on each and every aspect of the mishap involving the T. F. Train. Eventually, the CEO sent word that such a detailed account of the train accident was not necessary. He further instructed the stationmaster to be briefer and just factual in the reports.

The very next time the T. F. train had trouble by running off the track near the Arrendale stretch below Tiger, the following message was sent to headquarters by the stationmaster: "Off again, on again, gone again!" And that was that!

# Miss Flossie's Memory Lives On

Over the years, a lady I dearly loved was Miss Flossie Wilkerson. This is an account of my memories of her life as a devoted daughter, an adoring aunt, a faithful church member, and a wonderful neighbor and friend.

Miss Flossie was born on March 22, 1896, the daughter of James M. and Georgia Frances McCurry Wilkerson, who were direct descendants of the earliest settlers in this county.

The family property was originally called Wilkerson Mountain, but is now know as Owl Mountain. I recall two of her siblings: a brother C.O. (Carnes Otto), who was called Carnie, and sister, Louise Wilkerson Carson. The walk from the homeplace to the old Tiger-Clayton highway took about twenty minutes. Mr. Jim daily walked to and from town to his clock, watch, and jewelry shop.

My sister, Peggy, as a teenager, has happy remembrances of visiting with Miss Flossie and her nieces as they walked to downtown Tiger on Sunday afternoon to enjoy a cold soft drink --not an "RC", not a "Big Orange", but the real deal--a bottled Coca-Cola!

In the fall of the year of 1922, a brother of Miss Flossie's, C.O., known as Carnie, and his new wife, Ethel Phillips Wilkerson, agreed to move with the Hurley family to central Florida to work in the citrus groves. (The Hurley family had long been part-time residents and large landowners here in Rabun.) Soon the wife, who was expecting their first child, became miserably homesick and grieved for family and familiar surroundings. Her husband Carnie assured her that as soon as she and the baby were able, the three of them would return to these mountains.

On February 21, 1923, a son was born. Sadly, the mother died during childbirth. Immediately, Miss Flossie, along with a nurse, traveled by train to Winter Garden, Florida, and returned with the infant nephew, who was named C.O. Wilkerson, Jr., but was called Phillip for his mother's family. Homeward bound on the same train was the casket bearing the mother, who is buried in the Clayton cemetery near the Baptist Church. His Aunt Flossie, Mama Fannie, and Papa Jim raised Phillip. When grown, he married Eva Ivester and named his first daughter Ethel for his mother and reared a family. Phillip passed away at the age of 46.

The most handsome couple I can ever recall seeing was Miss Flossie and her fiancé, Ernest Dotson. During their courtship, the two regularly attended the old Tiger Methodist Church. The last time I saw this happy twosome was at an evening revival meeting. I listened intently to the plans for a wedding to be held just as soon as Ernest was discharged from the CCC Camp. Tragically, Ernest died from complications of spinal meningitis on January 6, 1937. Instead of a happy wedding day, there was a sad funeral.

Ernest Edward Dotson was buried at the Antioch Methodist Church cemetery. Miss Flossie grieved for the rest of her life, remaining true to her beloved, and over the years, she always kept flowers on the gravesite. She died on September 11, 1991 at 95 years of age. Her final wishes were granted as she was laid to rest next to the grave of Ernest.

I have heard reports of ghostly sightings on the old wagon road on Wilkerson Mountain. One tale is that by the light of the full moon, as the mist rises, two shadowy figures have been observed -- a tall stately woman briskly walking as a boy-child skips happily near her side. Maybe this is only an optical illusion of Miss Flossie and Phillip?

At other times as the apple blossoms float about in the soft night breeze, the vague outline of a couple is seen strolling, hand in hand, down the path. Some even say that barely audible musical notes of "Let Me Call You Sweetheart" have resounded through the woods. Is this a mirage of Miss Flossie and her lost love, Ernest?

As a winter blizzard of snow creates a wonderland of white, there are brief glimpses of Mr. Jim and Mrs. Fannie as a newlywed couple; he age 18 and she only age 14, as they journey towards the home-place to begin a married life together for the next 66 years. Yes, is this imagination, or is it a true likeness?

# A Tribute to the Class of 1947!

*The month of May is a time of busy activities, of making wedding plans, of honoring mothers, of organizing family gatherings, and yes- -even class reunions! On May 26, 2007 the Rabun County High School Class of 1947 will celebrate their 60th year reunion. To honor my fellow graduates, I shall recall memories and happenings over this time beginning on May 26, 1947, until the present time.*

Graduates exercises for the Seniors of 1947 were held on the evening of May 26 in the old high school auditorium. The commencement speaker was the late H. Grady Garrard, Superintendent of the Hall County School; and the topic of his address to the class of 1947 was "What Will You Do With Your Life?" Wearing the traditional red and white caps and gowns, the twenty-nine graduates listened intently.

In the autumn of 1947, the graduates went their separate ways, some to various occupations locally, others to attend vocational schools or college. Several migrated to employment at the automobile plants in Michigan. Two of the "grads", Claude E. Powell and Robert "Sonny" Dixon were veterans of World War II and have now resumed civilian life. Clyde Hill, Jr. immediately entered the business world, and has been very successful in merchandising.

1950-1952: During the Korean Conflict, service men from Rabun County included the following graduates of the Class of '47:

Roane Arrendale
John W. Baker
John A. Carter
Robert "Bob" Crunkleton
R. E. "Rainbow" English
Robert H. Floyd
Leroy "Roy" Garland
J. Coleman Jarrard
Frank C. Marsengill
Robert "Bob" Massee
William "Bill" McClain
Thomas H. Ramey
Truett Thompson
George P. Yarn

Later, James E. Bleckley became a Naval officer after completing medical college.

These men, serving in the military forces, received much recognition. Each was a tough, hardy mountaineer who could withstand the perils of battle and who took pride in serving his country. Returning home, these men became builders, farmers, contractors, engineers, mechanics, utility workers, and electricians in this area.

1953: The members of the Class of 1947 were most grateful when the vaccine to prevent polio was developed as Ted Parker had been a polio patient. He was severely disabled, but with his crutches, his determination, and his smile, Ted graduated with this class in 1947. Too, we admired James Lee Ramey, who had a crippled arm due to a birth injury. He overcame this obstacle and received a degree in textile engineering from Georgia Tech.

1967: The nine "sweet girl graduates" are, by this Mother's Day, homemakers, wives, parents, even working mothers--who are living in and around this mountain region. They are:

Helen Cannon (Hunter), Leo Craig (Smiley), Elise Donaldson (Fields), Janie Pleasants (Taylor), Ruth Queen (Smith), Janet Smith (Segars), Bobbie Faye Teague (Bleckley), Madalene York (Stanton), and Mildred York (Hogsed)

1976: When a Georgia native, Jimmy Carter, became President of the U.S., I recalled the class trip to Washington, DC. The Class of 1947 was the first Rabun County High School senior class to have a school-sponsored educational field trip to the nation's capital. During the nine days there, we toured the historic sites, visited places of interest, and viewed the government in action. We had a very special "tour guide", our classmate. Tom Ramey, had served as a Page for three months in the US House of Representatives at the Capitol. To my knowledge, he is the only student in the history of Rabun County High School to be appointed a Page to Congress.

1995: As the Atlanta Braves won the World Series, I clearly remembered that in the spring of 1947, Rabun County High School fielded the very first baseball team. Wearing brand-new baseball uniforms, the seniors played a winning schedule. One classmate, Ralph Swanson, had two loves of his life: his wife Myron and BASEBALL!

In 1947, there was no football program at Rabun County High School. However, basketball players, on both girls' and boys' varsity teams with the Seniors of '47, had won championship games. For the very first time, Rabun County High School cheerleaders were chosen from the class of 1947, and "the school spirit" could be heard loud and clear!

2007: Sixty years later, the Class of 1947 can truthfully answer the question posed by the late H. Grady Garrard on graduation night: "What Will You Do With Your Life?" These Seniors have been committed to their family members, dedicated church, civic and community leaders, and productive citizens. Yes, Dr. Garrard, the Rabun County High School Class of 1947 has "done good".

We offer special recognition to the graduates of the class of 1947 who have gone on before us.

Rabun County High School graduating class of 1947

# Ms. Zella, my First Grade Teacher

A most respected and beloved teacher, friend, and neighbor, Mrs. Zella Crawford Ramey recently left her earthly home to dwell with the Heavenly Host. No one ever deserved the angel wings and halo more than she.

When I was a first-grade student at the old white Tiger schoolhouse (seventy-one years ago in 1936), Ms. Zella was the teacher who taught me not only to read, but to love the printed word. During this first year of schooling, my front baby teeth would become loose. Ms. Zella would painlessly remove the "wiggly" small tooth. During the summer vacation, I would cry and beg for Ms. Zella to pull the dangling, wobbly tooth. So, Mama or Daddy would take me to the front porch of the Crawford home in Tiger for a "dental visit", and she never accepted any payment for the extraction of eight baby teeth.

This demonstrates the care and concern that Ms. Zella had for each and every pupil. I recall that prior to the lunch period each day, we recited the simple prayer of thanks:

"God is great. God is good.

Let us thank Him for this food."

Ms. Zella, with her sweet disposition, patience, kindness, and compassion, left a wonderful legacy, twenty students at a time, for thirty-seven years. Truly, teachers lay the foundation on which all other professions are built.

Ms. Zella also had the creative gift of handiwork. This natural ability was evident in the delicate tatting lace doilies which she made and shared with many of us. A tatting shuttle and thin thread are used to create a series of intricate knots; Ms. Zella taught me to read and to write, but I could not learn the art of tatting. She tried, and I tried, but to no avail. I cannot tat.

A favorite memory for many of us was seeing Ms. Zella tending the flowers in her yard. The blue hydrangeas, the red "rooster combs", the white Ressurection lilies, and the pink asters were among her favorites.

Ms. Zella was a native of Rabun County, born to Julia Ella Holcomb and Martin Crawford on October 27th, 1911, and she died on October 12th, 2006, just fifteen days before turning 95 years of age. Her sister, Della Crawford Watts, was four years older, and these two sisters were best friends, close neighbors, and loving, supportive "kindred spirits" their entire lives.

Ms. Zella graduated from Clayton High School and finished at Piedmont College. She taught school at Tiger, Persimmon, and Tallulah Falls. She married Bell Ramey and they had a son, Crawford C. Ramey. As a single parent, Ms. Zella raised and educated her child. To her delight, Crawford and his wife (the former Maureen Bramlett) retired back home to Rabun after years of residing in Douglasville and in Pennsylvania.

Ms. Zella was not famous; she didn't make the five o'clock news nor the headlines of a daily paper. She didn't write books. Instead she taught hundreds of us to read and appreciate them. Ms. Zella had a successful life and she truly made this corner of the world a better place to live.

Now, up in Heaven, the angel robes are edged with delicate tatting lace, the Heavenly Garden is aglow with the "fall pinks" and other flowers, and the younger angels are gathered around Ms. Zella as she reads the beloved Mother Goose rhymes and Bible stories -- just as I did when I sat in her classroom long ago.

---

Janie Pleasants in the 1st grade

# Bonding

My husband, John Melvin, was born in October, 1925. His first cousin, Winnie Garland, was born three months earlier in August of that year. Both were strong, healthy infants, and both have just celebrated their 80th birthdays!

As Thanksgiving Day approached that Fall in 1925, Aunt Nora, the mother of Winnie, needed to go to town. By walking, or by riding in a horse-and buggy, it was an all-day trip.

Mrs. Minnie, who was the mother of Melvin, offered to keep the three-month old Winnie. As the hours went by, both Melvin and Winnie became very fretful and restless. Mrs. Minnie tried to appease the two crying infants by fixing a "sugar tit", which is a bit of butter, covered with sugar, and tied up in a soft cloth. Neither baby took to this substitute at all! (Remember that in 1925 no infant formula nor baby bottles were available.)

Then, Mrs. Minnie decided that she had two whining babies, and that nearby and available were two "dinner bags". She began nursing her son, Melvin, and her niece, Winnie, at the same time -- one on each side!

The worried Aunt Nora arrived and gave a deep sigh of relief for Mrs. Minnie was rocking and softly singing to two sleeping babies nestled on each shoulder. The first cousins had full tummies and happy hearts. Truly, this was "bonding" in the truest sense of the word!

---

Mrs. Minnie Taylor

Mrs. Minnie's charges,
Melvin and Winnie, in 2008

# The Keeping Room

M ost of the early settlers in these mountains lived in one-room log cabins. The main area was called the keeping room. The fireplace served as a place to cook, provided heat and warmth, and was the only source of light. After the busy day, the family members gathered around. The girls and women did needed handiwork such as knitting, quilting, and weaving. The men folks "whittled" or did wood carving, to create needed wooden tools or play toys for the children who were sleeping in the loft above.

Over recent years, Shannon Garland Alley and I have been "resource persons" for the Elder hostel program. This original poem, "The Keeping Room" has always been a favorite of natives and visitors alike. I am sure that you, the Laurel readers, will enjoy and appreciate this descriptive poetry by Shannon.

### The Keeping Room  by Shannon Alley, 1990

In the keeping room at my granny's house, The treasures bring to mind,
All the loving memories, Of a journey back in time...
The antique trunk holds treasures and thoughts unfold anew,
Like the satin pillow covers from brother, sent home from World War II...
There are aprons, a tatting shuttle and photographs of generations gone behind
That express the solemn dignity of another age and time...
See the fragile wedding dress stitched with love and pride
To enhance the virginal beauty of a young and blushing bride...
The beautiful heirloom cameos, lovingly wrapped in such a way
To be saved for a future daughter's sacred wedding day...
First born child's baby sacques, and a faded Christening dress
Once knew a mother's loving care and felt her soft caress...
The delicate china tea set given to granny at baby's birth
Could never be replaced for the memories that it's worth...
There are handkerchiefs and pillow slips and auntie's dresser runner,
A knitted cap to keep out the cold of a lone and weary hunter...
Papa's white iron bedstead, stands so strong and high
With coverlets and homemade quilts for warmth in years gone by...
"Let not your heart be troubled" reads a sampler on a wall,
And all the tables are adorned with lace and hand made shawls...
In a rocking chair by the fireplace the warmth makes me sigh,
There are tea towels hanging on a line someone hung to dry...
Yes, Granny's keeping room is special with lasting memories to be found
For here you feel her love that lingers all around.

# Ms. Mary and the Weavers of Rabun

Among my collection of "old-timey" items native to this area I have a treasured piece of woven material 60"x90" size, indigo-violet-blue in color. The fabric is hand-loomed of linen and woolen yarn; the pattern is an intricate geometric design with distinctive border. My question is, "Can this beautiful coverlet be an authentic creation by the "Weavers of Rabun" at the Hambidge Center some twenty years ago?" When I look at this textile work of art, I recall the following: Whenever the late Mary Hambidge needed help with ailing sheep or had concerns about a timber disease, she would summon my Granddaddy Arrendale, a former county agent, for advice and assistance. With excitement, I went along! We would travel in an old 1934 Ford car through Tiger, up to Clayton, through Mountain City, on to Dillard, and turn left on Betty's Creek Road. Then, we bounced along the dirt road four miles to the establishment know as the Center.

Here I was fascinated by the activities. The wool was sheared from the sheep on the farm, washed, carded to remove any briars or bits of leaves, and then placed on the spinning wheel to become yarn. Then the skeins of the wool thread were dyed with natural materials such as plant roots, berries, hulls, bark and leaves, resulting in beautiful colors. The next step was to thread the loom according to a specific pattern and the weaving process began. Perhaps as many as 15 looms were busy at one time. The ladies who were weaving were neighbors and kinfolks from this area.

A most amazing person, Mary Hambidge was tiny in size with long red hair. She wore the most unusual dresses of woven material, and her long knit stockings were worn during all seasons of the year! Later, I realized that her outfits were made of the same fabrics being sold on Fifth Avenue in New York City! The "Weavers of Rabun" were known internationally for their originality in design and expert workmanship.

Most importantly, I remember being seated on the steps of the porch at the Rock House and listening to my Granddaddy and Mary Hambidge discuss, at length, the need to protect and preserve the beauty of these mountains for future generations to enjoy. Thus, my first lesson in ecology!

Even with this flashback in years, the mystery remains as to the true source of my cherished possession -- the woolen coverlet. But, for all practical purposes, I shall consider the original work of art as being created by the skillful "Weavers of Rabun". Why not?

# Truth or Fiction?

Some interesting information concerning my Arrendale heritage is that Thomas Arrendale, the original settler, was sent to England as a young man to study engineering. When he returned to the new country, he decided that this career was not his "cup of tea" so Thomas migrated from South Carolina, crossing over the Chattooga River, and settling in the area of Burton. Family history relates that Thomas fought in the War of 1812; but is it the truth that he and his Indian orderly, Gold Tooth, were really heroes in the Battle of New Orleans? True or not, it makes for a most interesting story.

One of his sons was Joel, my great great grandfather. Family information reveals that Joel Arrendale had three brothers who joined the Gold Rush to California to mine the precious metal. I've always heard that one son returned to Burton but his bag of gold nuggets was stolen, one drowned in the Mississippi as he traveled East, and one was said to settle elsewhere. But, who knows for sure?

The Arrendale family owned hundreds of acres of land. Joel's son Martin, my great grandfather purchased the house and land where I was raised.

Sometime in the late 1800's a cousin, William Arrendale, was unjustly accused of the serious crime of manslaughter. Rather than being convicted and sentenced to the dreaded underground gold mine prison in Dahlonega, William decided to evade the law and escaped to the West. One can only imagine his sadness as this Arrendale male stood at the top of Glassy Mountain and, for the last time, viewed his inheritance. Over the following years, he was not heard from and was presumed dead.

Then a telephone call came to my Granddaddy Arrendale which was from the son of the long-lost cousin, William. A report was given that William, on his death bed, told his family of the events leading up to his arrival in Oregon. He had assumed the surname "Russell", his mother's maiden name, and had been most successful in the business world. The dying man's last request was that his Arrendale kinfolk back in Rabun County, Georgia be contacted to inform them of his survival and life story. Can truth be stranger than fiction?

---

# Navy Corpman to the Rescue

Each and every vet has a "tale to tell" and this is a brief account of the wartime activities of my husband, Melvin John Taylor. After being drafted in December, 1943, Melvin was no longer a senior class member at R.C.H.S. but a Navy recruit at the Great Lakes, Illinois Naval Center. There he was selected to receive instruction and develop skills as a medic. Next, at Camp Pendleton, California, Melvin completed both the Field Medical School and combat training.

Immediately, Navy Corpsman Taylor was assigned to the First Marine Division and within days he shipped out for overseas duty in the Pacific where fierce fighting with Japan was continuing. (The Navy white outfits were mailed home to Rabun County. Melvin proudly wore the Marine uniforms for the remainder of his tour of duty.) After the troops completed maneuvers in the Soloman Islands, the Okinawa campaign began on Easter Sunday, April 1, 1945, and the bitter combat lasted for 87 terrible days.

As the company aid man, Melvin cared for the wounded and comforted the dying Marines. A constant fear was the Japanese Kamikaze (or suicide) planes and their attacks. One incident that Melvin recalls took place just three days prior to the end of the Okinawa conflict. While Melvin was moving an injured Marine to be transferred on to the field hospital, another Jeep ambulance carrying the body of General Simon B. Buckner who, just an hour before, had been mortally wounded by enemy fire drove up to Melvin's collecting station.

As a memorial to this respected and admired troop commander, the nearby body of water, partly enclosed by the island of Okinawa, is named Buckner Bay. After the surrender of Japan on August 15, 1945, the First Marine Division was ordered to "China duty". They were to serve as occupation forces in North China. Unloading at the mouth of Pei Ho River, the troops were transported by barges. Tugboats towed them up to the city of Tientsin.

Melvin along with a group of Marines was on the last barge. For three days and three nights, the squad watched and waited for the tugboats to return. By now, their food supply was totally exhausted. As the guys were becoming hungrier and more restless, Melvin walked onto the sloping shores to a nearby Army supply depot. When he asked for the needed food, the mess Sergeant rudely informed Melvin that it was necessary to have a requisition from an officer to secure rations. The Sergeant was unconcerned when told there was no officer on the barge. Looking down the beach, Melvin saw two men walking. One appeared to be a Navy Officer with "scrambled eggs" on his cap; the other looked like a Marine officer.

Rushing toward the officers, Hospital Apprentice First Class Melvin John Taylor saluted and then "his shoes sunk two feet into the sand" for he was face-to-face with Brigadiere General Louis R. Jones, Chief Executive Officer of the First Marine Division!

Without hesitation, Melvin asked for assistance, and his leader said, "Go tell the Sergeant that General Jones said to provide your troops with the needed food supplies."

The Sergeant had observed this encounter and, needless to say, boxes of 10-1 rations were ready and waiting for the Marines. Eventually, the tugboats returned, and the barge moved north. After two years, two months, and eighteen days in service, Melvin was discharged and returned home to his native mountains. In the words of his father, Renard Leamon Taylor, "Melvin left as a boy and returned as a man."

---

A young Melvin Taylor

161

# Peggy and Albert's Wedding

It was the spring of 1959. Mama Clyde and my sister, Peggy, had planned to go on a long anticipated trip to Europe. Aunt Ruth and Uncle Trimble (Col. Ezzard) were stationed in Germany. However, Peggy was "in love" with Albert and did not want to go. She chose instead to go to summer school at the University of Georgia. Albert was a co-op student at Georgia Tech and was scheduled to attend summer school, also.

They had a great summer as they dated each week-end. I was their chaperone and I had a busy summer!

Mama returned from overseas, having had the European tour of her dreams. She became exasperated with Peggy's tears each Sunday when Albert left and said, "If you are that much in love, why don't you just get married?" Mercy, Peggy couldn't believe her ears! Excitedly, they planned for a December wedding.

A week later when Mama Clyde was attending a vocational education meeting in Atlanta, Peggy and Albert sat in Piedmont Park and came up with an earlier marriage plan that might be approved by their parents. There were a lot of "IFs" - IF Peggy could get in a college in the Atlanta area instead of Fall quarter at the University of Georgia (she was admitted to Oglethorpe University), IF they could find a place to live (they bought a WWII vintage 28 foot trailer), IF they could find a cheap car (they did, a green 1952 Chevrolet with a cracked engine), and IF they could plan and carry off a wedding in three weeks!

They picked Mama Clyde up from the meeting and shared their plan - she bought it on the condition that Miss Lorraine and Mr. Albert did! Then she said, "Oops, if we are going to have a wedding, we must stop by Lenox Square (which had opened that summer) and get a pattern and material for your wedding dress." They went to Rich's fabric department and found the perfect pattern and Skinner satin for the dress which was to be trimmed in lace that Mama had brought from Belgium. They found Peggy's satin shoes and went into the big Kroger to get nuts for the reception!

Then on to Clarkesville to see Albert's parents. They agreed to the scheme and the push was on!

Peggy and Mama had bought lovely note paper for the proposed

December wedding. They became hand written invitations. Sue Roane Duckworth, Miss Lorraine, Peggy, and I wrote invitations that Sunday afternoon in late August.

Mama's school started that week. Peggy made her wedding dress, Albert had his finals at Georgia Tech, Mama planned the reception, Miss Lorraine planned the cake & mints, and they attended to all the "IFs"!

The wedding week-end arrived. Albert took down a fence in front of Mama's house to enable reception guests to park. In the process he got into some poison ivy or schumake and had an allergic reaction with swollen hands and some on his face.

The Thrashers hosted the delicious rehearsal dinner at their home in Clarkesville. Then off to Tiger Methodist Church for the rehearsal. The minister was a distant cousin of ours and was serving a church in Bethlehem, Georgia. The rehearsal went well.

Sunday, September 13, 1959 was a beautiful, very warm Fall day. The groom's best man was his father, Albert Sr., Peggy was "given away" by our Uncle John Arrendale Jr., I was Peggy's Matron of Honor, Albert's brother, Roy, was one of the ushers. Miss McKinney (Peggy's elementary principal) was the pianist, Mrs. Anabel Donaldson (Peggy's high school English teacher) was to read Robert Burn's Sonnet "How Do I Love Thee?", and Mrs. Philp was to sing the Lord's Prayer.

As guests were seated in the small sanctuary of the freshly painted church, Miss McKinney was playing a selection of songs. Albert and his father were sequestered in a small airless Sunday school room where the windows had been painted shut. Guests noticed that Miss McKinney began playing selections repeatedly as 4:30 came and went. The minister from out of town had NOT arrived!

Thankfully, the Dillard - Mountain City charge preacher, Julian Scott, was to be in attendance and arrived late. Mama told him that his services would probably be needed, to which he replied, "I don't have my Discipline!" Grandma Arrendale always kept her Discipline (a book of Methodist rituals) on top of the piano, so Mama sent Henry Ezzard in Granddaddy's old red farm truck to get the book. Still no preacher who had conducted the rehearsal!

A few minutes later, Henry arrived with the book and the emergency preacher went back to the hot Sunday school room. He shook hands with both Alberts and said, "This is my first wedding!" Then he looked to the heavens and said, "May the good Lord bless us all."

Bless his heart, he was so frightened. He didn't know what was planned at the rehearsal. He did a grand job. After he pronounced them as "man and wife" he looked at Albert and whispered, "Are you going to kiss the bride?" To which Albert responded in a voice that was heard in the back of the small church, "Damn right I am!"

The lovely reception was at Mama's house. The out-of-town minister made it to the reception with apologies and humility. They had gotten behind a funeral procession that traveled a long distance on the two-lane roads of the 1950's.

About the time Peggy had changed into her "going away" outfit, Julian Scott came dashing into the reception to give Albert a "Certificate of Marriage". Bless him, he had gone to the parsonage in Dillard to get it signed and delivered!

After the honeymoon on a cousin's houseboat on Jackson Lake, they completed their college years and had very successful careers. They have two children and two grandchildren. In their retirement, they have returned to Tiger to enjoy their "golden years" in "God's Country"!

---

Albert and Peggy P. Thrasher

# The Heirloom Pump Organ

From my mother I inherited a reed pump organ, the matching swivel stool, and an instruction book for students of the organ. Older family members recall that this musical wind instrument arrived in Rabun County around 1918. My mother had bottle-fed and raised a Jersey heifer calf which she sold and the cash money was used to buy this much desired organ. It was purchased from the Major Bryan McDowell family of the Cartoogechaye community of Macon County, North Carolina, and was shipped from Franklin to Tiger on the old Tallulah Falls Railroad. Next by horse and wagon, the organ was hauled to the Arrendale homestead where it remained until 1933. The organ was moved to Mother's white house on the north side of Tiger where it has remained in the same room, safe and protected, for the past seventy-one years. I have been told that at one time a family of mice nested in the organ bellows, but repairs were made by Uncle John Edwards prior to his death in 1932.

The organ was first believed to have been imported from England, but this was incorrect. It was built by the Jacob Estey Company in Vermont, which operated from 1848 to the mid 1950's. The rich mahogany frame is 55 1/2" in height, 24" in width and 48" in length. The wood carvings are of a simple design; there are no mirrors. A small round shelf is situated on each side for candles or kerosene lamps to be placed for a source of light. When the organ lid was raised, the nine stops and the keyboard (with 25 black keys and 36 white keys) can be seen. The antique three-legged stool has a foot square seat cushioned in maroon velvet upholstery. There are two foot pedals which must be pushed, fast and furiously, to create a vacuum for the musical sounds to be produced. Both amateur and professional musicians have played this organ with renditions of beloved tunes and hymns such as "The Lily of the Valley", "The Old Rugged Cross", "Amazing Grace", "Silent Night", and "America".

This old organ has witnessed many family events and happenings, including times of joy (as with the births of my brother Jim and sister Peggy), periods of illness and the sadness of death, the excitement of birthdays, "Family Feeds", graduations and weddings of four generations of kinfolks -- and has observed more quilting parties than the keys on the keyboard!

My mother, Clyde Ellen Arrendale, believed in the heritage of the heirloom and such a tradition must be maintained. Mother's first great grand-daughter, Whitney Ellen Ray, became her namesake. Because she was named for my mother, I shall pass with love and affection the treasured organ, stool, and book on to Whitney Ellen. She is to be married to Leland Cox in the coming spring and her "dowry" will be the inherited parlor organ. The organ will be moved over the mountain and valleys to Lumpkin County, Georgia where it will have a place of honor in the new home of Whitney Ellen and Leland. Once again, the soft and melodious sounds will render another chapter to be in the journal of travels and tales of the old family organ.

Janie P. at the organ

# The Yankee Horse

John Crawford Edwards was my great Grandfather. His daughter, Tallulah Edwards Arrendale, was my grandmother. My mother, Clyde Ellen Arrendale Pleasants English, was her daughter. My great Grandfather was born in 1833 in Virginia. He had seven children before the war (six others after returning home from the war). He was assigned to Company A, Georgia 11th Battalion of the Light Artillery. He served as Quartermaster, responsible for housing for the CSA officers and men, and distribution of provisions for several companies. After a short time, he was promoted to Acting Quartermaster for the Brigade commanded by General John Bell Gordon.

Grandpa Edwards was present at Appomattox in April 1865. Now according to family history, Grandpa Edwards was mustered out of the defeated CSA on the day of the surrender. Having no means of transportation, he began the long walk home to Smarr in Monroe County, Georgia. That evening, as he rested by a cool watering hole, he was joined by a Federal soldier driving a wagon who was on route to Ohio. The two former enemies engaged in polite then friendly conversation. They discussed how important it was to hurry home to get the crop in the ground.

The Yankee soldier asked, "Where are you going, Reb?"

"Home to Georgia," replied Grandpa Edwards.

"Where's your mount?" asked the Yankee.

"Haven't got a mount. I'm traveling by foot," answered Grandpa.

Upon pondering this, the kindly Yankee said, "Well, you'll never get home in time to get that crop in the ground. I'll just divide my team of horses with you! I'll keep ole' Pat and you take Beck on with you!"

So, the Yankee soldier, dressed in blue, drove his horse and wagon to home and family in Ohio; the Rebel soldier, dressed in tattered gray, traveled south to home in Georgia on his gift horse. The only farm animal that Grandpa had to make a crop and feed his family that season.

In the last years, Grandpa Edwards lived with our family and often talked about the kindly Yankee and the Yankee horse. He always wondered if the Yankee made his way home to Ohio. Grandpa died in 1922 and is buried in the Tiger Cemetery in Rabun County under the gray CSA tombstone.

# John Patrick Pleasants

In a peaceful country cemetery lays a tiny grave with a headstone which reads "John Patrick Pleasants" and the little girl within me remembers:

In the fall of the year of 1930, I was born to Clyde Ellen Arrendale and Miles Otis Pleasants. As was the medical procedure at that time, my mother remained at the hospital for two weeks after delivery. In 1933, my mother was expecting again. I knew she would be absent for several days and then she would bring the new baby home. I was totally prepared for the arrival of a brother or sister; however, I was not prepared for the news that the baby boy, John Patrick, had died at birth and would not be coming home to live with us. Then, the infant clothes and crib were quietly put away. In 1936, my brother, Jim, was born and in 1939 my sister, Peggy, joined our family circle.

Throughout my young years and into my adulthood, I would occasionally dream of my little brother. He grew, changed, and always appeared to be two years younger than me in my dreams. As the dream ended, I would always receive a message that John Patrick had died. Then I would awake sobbing and screaming. My folks referred to this as "Janie P's nightmares". I never revealed to anyone the source of my tears and sadness.

Shannon Garland Alley lost a son in 1991. As she worked through her grief, I shared with her this account of my loss and the recurring dream. Later on that cold wintry night when sleep would not come, Shannon wrote the following poem:

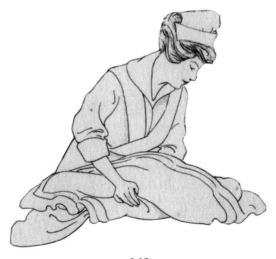

# John Patrick: Born and Died, 14 August 1933

My little brother died on the day he was born,
I never felt the grief because I was too young to mourn.
A vision of a small gray coffin whispered through my mind
And the absence of my brother bewildered me at times.
I never saw his face or the sweet things he might do
For the year that he was born and died, I was only two.

Then, in a dream one night, I saw him toddle through the door!
By his dimpled cheeks and baby curls, he was two and I was four!
One night, I saw him, bigger now, swing on a gate.
His baby look was gone for he was six and I was eight.

Once I saw him running and his energy knew no end,
He always kept right up with me though I was twelve and he was ten!
We were so very close as we grew into our teens
For we'd grown up together -- if only in my dreams!

You see, I always slept expectantly and awoke so terrified
For in every dream, in a different way, my brother always died!
I would cry and tremble as his life would then unfold
And for reasons I still don't understand, I never told a living soul.

He came one night, in a uniform, proudly going off to war,
He seemed reluctant, this time, to leave, more than ever before,
Then, I heard a shot, felt the pain -- and John Patrick was no more!

In time, I had a baby girl and oh, I loved her so!
I lavished her with all the love John Patrick never lived to know!
I wanted him to know such love, but I waited long in vain,
I guess, somehow, he already knew, because, he never came again.

Much research has been conducted on the emotional effects of sibling loss and the way in which children deal with this loss. Until recently, I had never encountered anyone who could relate to my nightmares. A lady in our Elderhostel audience revealed that her brother died in WWII and that the two of them had grown old together in her dreams. Lately, they both are drawing their Social Security checks!

# Turning the Table on the Storyteller

Long before the written word was available to record the past and preserve it for the future, there was the art of storytelling. It's an art that has, in too many cases, become relegated to the antiquity of the rotary dial telephone and the black and white TV.

Believing that storytelling is an integral part of our mountain heritage, *The Georgia Mountain Laurel* magazine and *Rabun's Laurel* before that, have always carried a monthly column by local Rabun County storyteller Janie P. Taylor.

The woman is an absolute fount of tales from the past, many of which poke fun at herself. And she's not above poking fun at others, particularly those with whom she can claim kin as kinfolks!

In true Janie P. form, the column she submitted for this issue dealt with the once, very necessary fixture in every back yard -- the outhouse. And it was a doozie of a column. The magazine staff, however, had other ideas, Janie P. We're going to save that classic tale for another time, and we're going to let some of your family tell tales on YOU!

This is your life, Janie P. Taylor!

\* \* \* \* \*

I am the oldest daughter, Judy W. Scott, teacher of young children for 34 years, who resides in Gainesville, Georgia. My children are Blake, 29 and Kelli, 26.

Traveling with Janie P. can best be described as an "Experience". In mid-July, a few summers ago, we planned a weekend trip to eastern North Carolina for the wedding of a cousin on the Pleasants side of the family.

After leaving Tiger early in the morn (and I do mean early), we motored thru Georgia and the Carolinas. Mom was "navigating" as I drove the scenic route. Because Mom left the driving to me, she was armed with the "cold hard cash", a current road map, and more than one pair of comfortable shoes!

Janie P. began being "helpful" early in our trip... and so the adventure really began. Whenever she made a suggestion or a directive was given, the following refrain was heard, "BUT YOU ARE THE DRIVER, SO DO WHAT YOU WANT."

170

"We may need a coke and to stretch our legs, BUT, YOU'RE THE DRIVER, SO DO WHAT YOU WANT TO DO."

"We may want to stop and fill up with gas, BUT, YOU'RE THE DRIVER, SO DO WHAT YOU WANT TO DO."

"You may need to tune in a local radio station for weather updates, BUT, YOU'RE THE DRIVER, SO DO WHAT YOU WANT TO DO."

"You may want to stop at a roadside stand for cantaloupe and peaches, BUT, YOU'RE THE DRIVER, SO DO WHAT YOU WANT TO DO."

You may need to slow down for the upcoming highway/road signs, BUT, YOU'RE THE DRIVER, SO DO WHAT YOU WANT TO DO."

Well, you get the picture and so it continued for hours and hours. The trip home? Same song, next verse, repeat refrain.

We have traveled together often since that summer -- always engaging in good conversation, looking for "Treasures" (stopping and shopping whenever we choose to do so), finding a good eatery, and always enjoying the sights. Never boring -- these journeys with Janie P.! I feel a "Road Trip" in the making and since I WILL BE DRIVING, I WILL DO WHAT I WANT TO DO!

........................................................................................

After the birth of my first child, Mom had said she was coming down for a weekend visit and bring food to cook to enjoy for several days. Very early Saturday morning (almost the middle of the night!) I heard strange, loud noises coming from my kitchen. After several minutes, I became concerned and decided to check out the source.

As I approached the front of the house, I saw a light on in the kitchen and heard pots and pans clattering. When I looked around the corner, there was Janie P. at the stove, busily preparing breakfast — and lunch and supper for a week! When I asked how she got in the house, she said she went to all the doors until she found one that was unlocked. Somehow the back door was left unlocked and in came Mom. To my surprise Janie P. had made herself at home about 6:00 AM with a cup of coffee!

* * * * *

I'm Becky Ray, Janie's middle daughter. My husband, Mike, and I have lived in Cornelia for the last 34 years since graduating from UGA. We are the proud parents of twin sons, Brooks and Vince, age 30, and a daughter, Whitney, age 27. We have three adorable grandsons, Preston and Parker Cox and V.J. Ray. A precious granddaughter arrived in January 2008 and she is my namesake, Kaleigh Rebecca Ray. Here's my story.

## The Shopping Trip

We were on a serious mission that quickly turned into a fashion frenzy. I am referring to a trip we made with my mother, Janie P. Taylor, to purchase the dress she would wear to the wedding of her oldest granddaughter, my daughter, Whitney Ray Cox.

It all started out simply enough. Whitney was behind the wheel and Mother was riding "shotgun". We daughters three were snugly buckled in the backseat. Wedding details were discussed as we motored down to the shopping center in Gainesville. Excitement was in the air as we laughed and "carried on" all the way down Hwy. 365.

We leisurely strolled into Belk's, but soon thereafter the pace quickened as we saw the dress department up ahead. We all but sprinted to the loaded racks of dresses that came into view as we turned the corner. (We hoped to find the perfect frock on the clearance rack -- preferably with an extra percentage off. Janie P. has always wanted the highest quality at the very lowest price.)

There we all were, whirling about and grabbing dresses, oblivious to other shoppers who innocently found themselves in our path. We were squealing with delight as we "oohed and aahed" over the dresses we thought might work. In the midst of all this flutter we sent Mother into the dressing room to put on the appropriate undergarments in order to insure a proper fitting. Time and space do not permit me to list all the layers of figure-flattering spandex Mother had brought along.

With our arms loaded with dresses of all colors and descriptions, we made our way to the dressing room to begin what ultimately would be considered a labor of love. Mother was ready and waiting with great anticipation as we showed her the stacks of dresses we had gleaned from the ladies' formalwear department.

We placed Mother in the middle of the three-way mirrored dressing room, and the elimination process began. The four of us surrounded Janie P. and instructed her to raise her arms and try to remain silent. There was no time for idle chatter as we pulled each dress over her head and down to the floor. We could tell almost immediately which ones would not make the cut. Those particular selections were on Janie P.'s body less than ten seconds each so as not to waste valuable shopping time. Any mention of a dress looking tacky, cheap, or flimsy meant it was no longer a possibility.

Of course, we all know most of us look better coming than going. This fact presented a challenge. Any dress worn in a wedding MUST look good from the back because that is the only view seen by most everyone present until after the ceremony. This fact weighed heavily on our minds. Absolutely, there could be no hanging threads, wadded fabric, or bulging seams as Mother walked down the aisle.

We continued to critique every dress until we all came to the point of complete mental and physical exhaustion. It was at that moment the bride-to-be Whitney said,"This is hysterical! Is this normal?" Janie P. quickly replied, "Absolutely not, but who wants to be normal?"

At long last, we all agreed on a gorgeous blue-gray silk creation with covered buttons and an embellished fitted jacket . Janie P. would float beautifully down the aisle as the maternal grandmother of the bride. Without a doubt, it was the right dress. It was the right style, the right color, and the right price. Above all, it was the one with the best view from behind.

Mission accomplished.

\* \* \* \* \*

My name is Dawne Bryan. As the youngest of the three girls, I married a "flat-lander", Randy Bryan and moved to the middle Georgia town of Cochran, where we raised our two sons—Zack, a civil engineer with a firm in Lawrenceville, and Beau, who, with his wife Katharine, resides in Augusta where he is a second year medical student at Medical College of Georgia. Having inherited the teaching gene, I am an educator teaching in Warner Robins, GA. We now have an "inside animal", our dachshund Maggie Mae.

# The Ghost Cat

There were times when our children were young that my husband and I would attend various insurance conventions. On one such occasion, Janie P. (or J.J. as she was affectionately known) was babysitting the boys. We had recently taken in a stray kittycat so she was also tending to our new pet. Having grown up in the mountains, it was understood that "animals belonged outside".

The first night Janie P. put the cat out as instructed and secured the door lock. The next morning, she awoke to find the cat inside. Mystified, she again put the cat outside, only to turn around and find it once again meowing at her feet. Now dubbed the "ghost cat", she put the varmint out once more. Five minutes later, he walked into the kitchen as calm as you please. Beginning to doubt her own faculties, she shooed him out. When he appeared inside only a few minutes later, she yelled, broom in hand, "I KNOW I put that cat out!"

We returned from our trip to find the children well but Janie P. agitated by her frequent run-ins with the "ghost cat". Determined to solve the mystery, I placed the cat outside and watched through the screen door. To my amazement, the kitten jumped into the dryer vent. I could hear him progress through the flexible dryer hose, where he exited, only a little rumpled, from a tear in the hose. Randy fixed the tear in the dryer vent hose and declared everything back to normal. We were able to assure Janie P. she was not losing her mind.

But, having enjoyed its excursions into the house, this was a determined animal. At the first opportunity, it jumped back into the vent. Only now its usual way was blocked. Cat wails could be heard as we all stood at the outside dryer vent pleading, "Here, kitty-kitty." Finally, the furry tail appeared and we were able to extract the animal. This time, Randy drilled holes and put wires inside the vent so no more varmints could climb in. Case (or shall we say, vent) closed.

There were many other J.J. babysitting visits, including one involving a golf ball, a tree, and our bird dog, but that's another story...

\* \* \* \* \*

I am Janie P. Taylor's youngest child and only son. My wife Karen and I along with our kids Renn, Arren, and Cami live in Habersham County.

As anyone who knows Janie P. will tell you, she loves a "do up" as much as anyone. Weddings, wedding showers, baby showers, receptions, anniversary parties, class reunions, family reunions, and all other types of similar affairs are just her "cup of tea". She has directed countless weddings over the years and witnessed hundreds more. In addition, she had a sterling silver punch bowl with matching tray, silver cups, and silver ladle (in the Paul Revere pattern) and all kinds of silver trays, fancy serving pieces, linen table clothes, lace coverlets, etc. that made up the remainder of the "do up in a box" kit for assorted occasions.

Many reading this article sipped non-alcoholic punch from her well used and extensively loaned collection. Janie P.'s stuff was used all over northeast Georgia and all she asked was that the borrower clean it up and put it back into the various boxes it came in. From the time I could be trusted not to drop the "silver punch bowl", I toted that stuff for mom and Ma Clyde down to the car, from the car to the event, and from the event back to the car, and the car back to the house. Since I became a driver (about 30 years ago), I have hauled punch bowls and silver trays to churches and reception venues throughout northeast Georgia for weddings, showers, anniversary celebrations, and any other "shindig" imaginable.

I did this with a glad heart and because Janie P. needed me to do it. Through the years, I have come to understand that Mom gets much enjoyment and great satisfaction from helping others with memorable events and being a part of the "do ups" and "shin digs" that memories are made of. Her love for a "do up" and the fact that she was a beloved teacher who taught every 8th grader in Rabun County High School for over 20 years have, no doubt, contributed to her notoriety. Almost everyone from 8 to 98 in Rabun County knows Janie P. and most will tell you they consider her a friend of theirs and their family. She is a wonderful mother and doting grandmother who is indeed a friend to all she meets.

\* \* \* \* \*

I'm Janie P.'s brother, Jim Pleasants. There is one matter which, without a doubt, others have told with more eloquence: When we were growing up, we took a lot of auto trips. These seemed never-ending, and Peggy and I were always relegated to the back seat, because Janie P. "got car sick" unless she was in the front seat. Years later, we learned that this malady was neither real nor psychosomatic; it was an intentional and despicable ploy to get that preferred front seat. This was a precursor to her later career as a storyteller.

I look forward to the surprise on Janie P.!

\* \* \* \* \*

I'm Janie P.'s sister, Peggy Thrasher. Janie was the first grandchild on the Arrendale side of the family. Being in this august position made her very special. On top of that, she was born in a hospital! Jim and I were born in the recently restored family home in "North Tiger". I refer to her as my "Big Sister" which doesn't always please her!

After Mama's death in 1999, Janie became the matriarch of our clan. She has assumed the role with vim and vigor. She will organize a birthday celebration or "family feed" on a moment's notice.

Our father, Miles Otis Pleasants, hailed from eastern North Carolina. He died in 1949. Mama made sure that we stayed in contact with our relatives, even those 400 miles away. In the distant past, the trips were very long -- a maximum of 45 mph during and at the end of World War II. Then came interstate highways. What a blessing, except that Janie was constantly backseat driving. Finally, after hearing, "That blue car has its blinkers on," or "The speed limit is 70," I told her that her only job while riding with me was to watch for I-85 signs and if she ever failed to see one to please let me know ! It worked!

Janie is a great correspondent. She has always been the best at remembering birthdays and getting cards mailed. In fact, we used to say that if she went to Athens she would send us a postcard! We have enjoyed cards from all over as she has attended conferences, family weddings, and traveled with her family.

For several years after she retired, Janie would hand paint with watercolors all occasion cards. The pictures were scenes from the mountains and so lovely. I have framed mine so we can enjoy them on and on. This hobby for which she is so talented has taken a"backseat" to quilting and writing for *The Laurel*!

Now, she thrives with her cellphone. She delights in checking on her family and friends.

Her birthday is quite a long celebration--remember she was the first born and first grandchild! Her birthday is in mid-November. She celebrates right through Thanksgiving to Christmas and thoroughly enjoys each card, call, gift, and visit. One October day several years ago, our brother Jim glanced at his calendar and thought," It's Janie's birthday!" He immediately called her with Happy Birthday wishes-- she appreciated the call especially when she informed him that he was a month early! To her advantage, Janie got to celebrate her birthday from mid-October through Christmas!

Janie is a great cook. To sit down at her table and enjoy a meal of her vegetables and cornbread is a treat. One cold winter Saturday, I made vegetable soup and called Janie and Melvin to come over and eat. When she said, "What can I bring?" I responded, "Cornbread, of course!" She brought not one but two pones of delicious cornbread. We had other guests from south Georgia. One man left with one of the pones and reported to me the next week that it was so good he had it for breakfast!

For years Mama had a quilting frame that could be lowered from the ceiling for her perpetual quilting parties. Apparently Janie got bitten by the "quilting bug" as she can be found daily quilting with her friends at the Rabun County Senior Center. She has quilted myriad colorful, warm, and decorative quilts that everyone cherishes.

When Janie wrote the Laurel story about "Back,backing up" on the highway, our daughter said,"Mama, has Aunt Janie no pride?" My response was that it has nothing to do with pride that Aunt Janie's storytelling is for her enjoyment and the entertainment of others. She accomplishes her goals well!

I recall four things about Janie P's principal's office at Clayton Elementary School. There was a lovely oil painting that Mama painted specifically for Janie's office--in fact, it hangs in my living room now. A rocking chair was there to comfort upset students and calm concerned parents. Then, there was a pretty cross-stitched sampler with a cow, fence, flowers, and this poem:

*The gum-chewing student*
*And cud-chewing cow*
*Look quite alike*
*But they're different somehow*

*And what is the difference?*
*I see it all now...*
*It's the intelligent look*
*On the face of the cow!*

When I became a principal, that sampler hung on my wall also!

Finally, there was a glass fish bowl that contained the names of classroom teachers on slips of paper. One of these was drawn each week and this teacher got to have a lunch break as Janie supervised that teacher's class in the lunchroom. This was years before "elementary duty free lunch" was mandated.

For many years during the 1940's and 1950's, Dr. J. C. Dover was chairman of the Rabun County Board of Education. In this position, he handed the high school graduates their diplomas. Since he knew most (if not all) of the families and graduates, he had a personal comment for each graduate. To Janie, he commented about her lovely smile and how far it would take her.

Indeed, her smile, her caring personality, her innate abilities, her painting, her quilting, her correspondence, her love of family, friends, and church; her talent for sharing our mountains through presentations and Foxfire, and her storytelling have made her a beloved Rabun Countian.

Our maternal grandmother, Tallulah E. Arrendale, exerted such a positive influence on our lives. At the conclusion of a service, meeting, or program she recited the Mizpah benediction and so, dear Reader, shall I:

*"The Lord watch between me and thee, while we are absent one from another." Genesis 31:49*

Our beloved Tiger Mountain

# Photo Gallery

Looking through the window to the pages ahead, there are photogaphs, past and present, of kinfolk and neighbors. They remind us of many memorable events and the traits of a mountaineer as named in the first article of this book. The people pictured exemplify the character, values, and beliefs of true mountaineers.

Janie P. and Melvin Taylor, wedding day, May 12, 1962

Janie P. Taylor

Left:  Melvin with friends, Lester J. Wall, on left, and Calvin Watts, on right, in 1946; and above with his son, Wesley, in 1964

Daughters Three in 1956
L to R: Judy, Becky, and Dawne

Wesley at age 3

Dawne Bryan, Judy Scott, Becky Ray,
and Wesley Taylor

Dawne W. Bryan and her family

Becky W. Ray and her family

Judy W. Scott and her
two children

Wesley Taylor and family

185

Clyde A. Pleasants:
as a baby, above;
as a young
lady, right;
and with her
great grandson,
Renn Taylor,
below

Above: Clyde A. and
Miles Otis Pleasants

Below: a treasured
picture of Janie P. of
her father's desk

Peggy P. Thrasher, Clyde A Pleasants,
Jim Pleasants, Janie P. Taylor

Peggy P.
Thrasher,
her daughter
Julielynn,
and son Al

Jim and Jeanne Pleasants and family

187

Granddaddy and Grandma Arrendale and children, Christmas, 1956

John V. Arrendale and wife Tallulah with children John Arrendale, Jr., Clyde Ellen, and Ruth Hanson Arrendale

Pictured L to R:  John V. Arrendale; his wife, Tallulah; his father, Martin Arrendale; and his sister, Lizzie Arrendale Baker

Grandma Tallulah holding Henry Ezzard with Lucy Ezzard (Bartlett) and kitty

The Taylors: Cami, Wesley, Renn, Karen, and Arren

The seven first cousins who grew up together at Tiger Mountain and Uncle Joe Arrendale. L to R: John Ezzard and Henry Ezzard; Second row: Lucy Ezzard Bartlett, Juncle Joe, Jim Pleasants; Top Row: Joanne Ezzard Barksdale, Janie Pleasants Taylor and Peggy Pleasants Thrasher

Melvin's grandfather, Lewis
Whitmire and his family

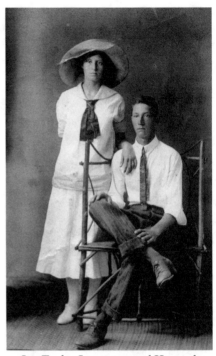

Iva Taylor Lawrence and Howard
Taylor, aunt and uncle of Melvin

Melvin's grandmother, Mary Page
Whitmire, and sons, Clint and Raymond

Carrie Taylor Hunnicutt and Iva
Taylor Lawrence, aunts of Melvin

Leamon R. Taylor,
Melvin's
father,
with his
pet mule

Minnie Henrietta
Whitmire Taylor,
Melvin's
mother,
at age 16

Melvin's
grandparents,
Jess and
Elizabeth
Taylor, and
family

Waunett Taylor Sexton, Melvin Taylor, Shelby Taylor Blackburn, Claudette
Taylor Bramlett, Allen Taylor, Ervin Taylor - Summer of 1984

Aunt Nora Taylor Garland and family
Front row: Wayne, Uncle Raliegh, Shannon, Aunt Nora,
and Laney    Back row: Allen, Winnie, Roy, and Lillian

Shannon Garland Alley
"The Tiger Poet"

Two Mountaineers:
Henry Ezzard and
Melvin Taylor

The Bartlett
Family:
Lucy (Ezzard),
Harry, William,
and Beverly
in 1962

Harry took the
pictures for
*The Storyteller*
cover.

The old
structure of
the Tiger
United
Methodist
Church where
so many fam-
ily members
were married,
baptised, and
had final
funeral
services.

Melvin "The Bean Man of Rabun" and Governor
Zell Miller at the Atlanta Farmer's Market, 1990

Melvin Taylor with his grandson and
namesake, Beau Taylor Bryan